I remember when Pastor Mike [   ] this encounter. I saw a rolled [   ] flying, so I knew it was not just a teaching but an impartation. The impartation is to bring us to a new understanding of our place and position of authority and to take authority over the second-heaven rulers of darkness.

KATHIE WALTERS
AUTHOR; SPEAKER; FOUNDER,
KATHIE WALTERS MINISTRY

I truly recommend you read Mike's book with a notepad and pen beside you. Read it slowly and look up the Bible references. You will be taken on a journey to better understand the invisible realm of God and learn how God's kingdom operates. I'm sorry to say this, but the average Christian today knows so little about godly authority. Don't be afraid to highlight or mark up the pages. Get ready because you are about to have your life changed like never before! I recommend not only reading this book but to start a discussion group also. Take a deep dive with others and explore third-heaven authority!

—DAN THOMPSON, PHD
PASTOR, FAITH BUILDERS FAMILY CHURCH
BANNING, CALIFORNIA

Third-Heaven Authority is *for you* if you've always wanted to learn the most and the best about the throne room of heaven from a person who has personally and intimately experienced it. Not only has Mike Thompson been caught up to the third heaven, but he's been especially gifted and anointed to write about it so you can "see it all," even without being caught up yourself. This book has already given me great revelation straight from the throne room that I'd never grasped before. Please buy it, and while you're at it, buy a copy for a friend too. It's that revelatory!

—STEVE SHULTZ
FOUNDER, ELIJAH STREAMS

THIRD-HEAVEN
AUTHORITY

MIKE THOMPSON

CHARISMA HOUSE

While the author has made every effort to provide accurate internet addresses at the time of publication, neither the publisher nor the author assumes any responsibility for errors or for changes that occur after publication. Further, the publisher does not have any control over and does not assume any responsibility for author or third-party websites or their content.

Visit the author's website at mikethompsonministries.org.

Cataloging-in-Publication Data is on file with the Library of Congress.
International Standard Book Number: 978-1-63641-159-0
E-book ISBN: 978-1-63641-161-3

3 2023
Printed in the United States of America

Most Charisma Media products are available at special quantity discounts for bulk purchase for sales promotions, premiums, fund-raising, and educational needs. For details, call us at (407) 333-0600 or visit our website at www. charismamedia.com.

I dedicate this book to CK, my loving wife and best friend. We continue to learn the ways of the Spirit together.

I'd also like to honor my father and mother, Edward and Lois, for passing on their spiritual legacy.

And finally, a special thanks to Max Davis, one of the many people who helped this book become a reality.

CONTENTS

FOREWORD

I CANNOT REMEMBER THE first time I encountered Mike Thompson, but I remember that it was my wife, Susanne, who introduced me to him via his videos. This was sometime in 2020, while we were all living through the bizarre nightmare of the COVID pandemic—and the increasingly authoritarian lockdowns that attended it. Most Americans with eyes to see knew something was amiss in our country, and very seriously so, and Mike Thompson's videos helped us to process what we were going through.

But I was immediately struck not just by what Mike Thompson was saying—which was encouraging and powerful and wise—but also by his demeanor in saying it. There was a positively compelling sobriety and matter-of-factness to him that made it obvious he was a seasoned man of God who understood the importance of what he was saying. There was none of the drama one sometimes finds in those who say things that fall under the term *prophetic*. There was a humility and a quiet joy—which evidenced a vital spiritual maturity—that infused whatever it was he was sharing and, of course, lent a deep credibility to what he said. Now that I've had the privilege of meeting him and his dear wife, CK, in person, I can say that those qualities are in evidence not just in the videos, which is of course precisely as I expected.

One might think that when God gives someone an especially rare anointing or gift He would also give them the character that such an extraordinary anointing or gifting requires. But time and again we are mystified to observe that that is not the case. We often see that whatever that anointing or spiritual gifting is in someone—whether in the prophetic or healing or whatever else—it can be seriously undermined by the lack of maturity we are sometimes saddened to find in the man or woman with that gift. But this was so dramatically not the case with Mike Thompson that I was unavoidably impressed and captivated and blessed.

Although he often shared some of the most amazing stories—of being caught up in the spirit and seeing visions—and even of warring in the heavenlies above the nation's capital—there was always a concomitant humility that was perfectly suited to the message that made it clear to whoever was watching and listening that Mike Thompson understood the almost unbearable responsibility that comes with having such an extremely important and rare gift—and with walking out that gift for God's purposes.

All of which brings me to the important subject of this important book: the idea that God in His infinite wisdom is calling His church to a more central role in engaging in spiritual warfare, and that Mike Thompson has been deputized by God to help us fathom what that role is and how we are to play our parts in fulfilling that larger role. It is these things of the spirit, of course, that are at the heart of all that happens in history. Historical events are but the visible layer of what is happening on a deeper and more central level, which is to say "in the spiritual realm." So if we care about God's purposes—and about the history through which we are living and which God calls us to participate in—then we are obliged to take God's call to us in this spiritual realm as seriously as possible.

While we are at it, let us never ever forget what a glorious privilege it is that the One who made the universe and created us in His image allows us to participate with Him in such things. We must be superlatively grateful to God, then, for this call—and for creating my friend Mike Thompson and calling him to lead us in that calling. I hope the Lord uses this book to help you become a vital part of the anointed, praying army that God is raising up in these last days for His purposes. God bless you! Amen.

—ERIC METAXAS
NEW YORK TIMES BEST-SELLING AUTHOR; SPEAKER;
HOST OF THE NATIONALLY SYNDICATED
ERIC METAXAS RADIO SHOW

CHAPTER 1

MY FIRST VISIT TO THE THIRD HEAVEN

PEERING OUT THE panoramic window of the penthouse suite, the city lights below appeared like sparkling jewels strewn across the dark fabric of night. Roars of intercession rose up around me from others gathered in this "upper room" as together we appealed to heaven. My wife, CK, and I had come to this city with about fifty other Christian leaders to intercede for an upcoming evangelistic crusade. The hotel conference center was in the process of setting up for the meetings that we were believing would usher in a great move of God in the city.

The manifest presence of God was thick in the room as we cried out for souls while warring against demonic strongholds. Praying in English and in other tongues, we decreed the word of the Lord together. In a moment of personal calm, while continuing to pray in the Spirit, I leaned against the wall and let my body slide down until I was sitting on the carpet. When I sat on the floor, an astounding thing happened. All the beautiful sounds of prayer, including my own, began to fade away, and in an instant I was caught up into the spirit realm.

No longer aware of the physical scene or activity around me, I felt myself lift up and out of the room! I knew I'd gone from the natural realm into the dimension of the spirit as I rose all the way through the ceiling of the suite and then the roof of the hotel. Continuing to ascend into the night sky, I now found myself looking down on the same city lights I had gazed at earlier.

Rising higher through the heavens, I could see numerous smaller lights hovering in the atmosphere over the city. These lights were dull, dingy, and reddish in color. No glory emanated from them, and I knew instinctively they were demonic spirits. Moving right through the dull lights, I suddenly found myself inside the throne room of heaven! Being caught up like this to heaven took me completely by surprise, yet there I was, standing in holy awe. What was most glorious, however, was that right in front of me was the Lord Jesus Christ sitting on His throne. I don't have the words to describe how magnificent the moment was. My words will be like a snapshot taken of the Rocky Mountains. They can't do it justice, yet I will try.

Angels surrounded Him on both sides, and nebulous silhouettes of other beings were behind the throne. They seemed slightly larger than the angels, and I wondered if these were the living creatures John described in his vision of heaven in Revelation 4:7–9. A canopy of swirling rainbow colors stretched over, above, and all around the throne. The colors were deep and rich, more radiant than anything on earth. Everything I was observing reflected the brilliance of the glory of God. As I tried to take it all in, my heart leaped, and joy overwhelmed me. Truly, "in [His] presence is fullness of joy" (Ps. 16:11).

Ezekiel's depiction of the rainbow surrounding the throne of the Lord immediately came to mind: "As the appearance of the rainbow in the clouds on a rainy day, so was the appearance of the surrounding radiance. This was the appearance of the likeness of the glory and brilliance of the LORD. And when I saw it, I fell face downward and

I heard a voice of One speaking" (Ezek. 1:28, AMP). John's account of heaven records a similar sight: "Encircling the throne there was a rainbow that looked like [the color of an] emerald" (Rev. 4:3, AMP).

And the music! I can never forget the music that permeated the atmosphere. The sounds of soft, peaceful music and voices were all around. Strangely, I couldn't distinguish the sounds because they weren't something I was accustomed to hearing on earth. The sounds were heavenly, making everything whole. All I can say is in heaven, everything worked together to produce a perfectly balanced environment.

It then occurred to me that I saw only one throne in front of me. I was puzzled at this for a moment because I expected to see two thrones—the throne of God and Jesus at His right hand. It was then that I heard a voice inside me quote Revelation 4:2: "Immediately I was in the Spirit; and behold, a throne set in heaven, and One sat on the throne." When I realized I was seeing the throne of Jesus, I was at peace.

As I gazed into the face of Jesus, I saw wisdom, strength, and compassion. I felt absolutely loved, accepted, and valued. I had never experienced such a feeling. There was no fear, no intimidation, no condemnation, shame, guilt, disapproval, inadequacy, failure, or self-doubt. All those things we struggle with here on earth were completely absent from my being. The revelation of complete love and peace had taken their place.

Inside, I could hear myself say, "Lord, is this who You created us to be? Is this what it feels like to be a new creation in Christ Jesus?" Then I realized that the hooks of the second heaven had completely come out of me. On earth, evil spirits seek ways to place hooks into the souls and flesh of believers. Through these attachments, the spirits attempt to influence the thoughts and behaviors of those believers. In heaven, I was standing before the Lord free, pure, and holy. Jesus didn't say a word as I contemplated all this. He simply allowed me to process what I was discovering. It was a precious, wonderful feeling.

The Holy Spirit, who was separate from Jesus, turned me around 180 degrees so my back was now to the throne of Jesus. From this view I saw a circular portal, about ten feet in diameter, before me on the floor. Through this portal, I could see the second heaven as well as observe the activities on earth. I looked all the way down to the intercessory prayer group below me. I could see the city they were praying for all around them. I also saw the numerous small, reddish demons that were in the atmosphere above the city but still below where I was in heaven. It was this group of demons that the prayer group was dealing with in the spirit.

Because of their earthly perspective, however, the prayer group could not see the full picture of what was happening above them. Looking down from heaven, I saw the whole spiritual battle from a completely different vantage point.

Then something else caught my attention. Above the reddish demons hovering in the air was a larger, dull, green light. I recognized this as another demonic being that seemed to be more powerful than the red ones below it.

This is when the Lord Jesus finally spoke to me. His words came from behind me because I was facing away from the throne, peering into this portal. "That's a general giving orders to the demons under him," He said. "They are following his orders. He is giving them the strategies and the commands."

Jesus continued, "Launch your warfare from here." At first I was surprised by His command. But then a holy boldness and authority rose up from inside me. "OK," I said, "I'm going to launch my warfare from here." I was ready to kick some demon butt and destroy every stronghold over that city!

Then I had a thought: "If I'm warring from heaven, do I need armor?" Again, the answer came as an impression in my spirit. I was reminded of Paul's depiction of the spiritual armor in Ephesians 6. I heard the Lord say, "You already know that the apostle Paul had a revelation of spiritual armor. Your understanding of who you are as a new creation is part of you on earth because it is a part of you in heaven." His words enlightened me, and I understood the armor as an integral part of our identity as new creatures in Christ.

More words began to come from behind me. Only this time, instead of just resonating inside me, these words came out my mouth. I looked down at that lead demon, the one that looked like a dull green light hovering over the smaller red lights. "In the name of Jesus," I boldly proclaimed, "I dislodge your assignment. I break every strategy. I break everything that you have set up against this city. I dismantle the communication structure between you and the lower-level demons, and I speak confusion into your ranks now!"

As I took authority over that general and the other demons, the angels standing in the throne room began to respond. When a command came out of my mouth, an angel on the right side shot down like lightning. Then

5

another angel on the left whooshed down as I spoke the next command.

I realized these angels were hearkening to the command of the Lord and to faith. Once they heard it, their job was to enforce the command given. As long as I was enforcing God's Word, the angels were enforcing my words.

This angelic activity went on for quite a while until I finished giving the commands. When it stopped, I stood there and looked around the throne room for several minutes.

MY ASSIGNMENT TO TEACH THIRD-HEAVEN AUTHORITY

To my surprise, Jesus stood up and walked over to me. With piercing eyes of pure love, He spoke these words: "I'm giving you the assignment to teach third-heaven authority to My people." This was the first time I had ever heard the phrase *third-heaven authority*, but Jesus explained what it meant. "We are now entering a season," He said, "when the veil between the physical realm and the spiritual realm will seem to get thinner. Believers will increasingly have more spiritual encounters. There will be visions and dreams, and they will become more prevalent. Believers will learn what it's like to operate in the Spirit and flow in heavenly things.

"However, this is universal in the spiritual realm, so demonic encounters will also increase in spiritism, the occult, mind science, and religions. It will also increase in people who just open themselves up to dark things." He then said: "Teach My children third-heaven authority so they will not be deceived by seducing spirits. They need to realize who I have created them to be and what they're capable of accomplishing. There needs to be credibility among those who learn to walk in the ways of the Spirit."

After that, Jesus began to illuminate the role of angels. "Angels are involved in every aspect of warfare, much more than you're aware of. Learn to depend upon them by letting them do their job. They respond to your authority." Then Jesus made this profound statement: "Third-heaven authority is about perspective, and only the Holy Spirit can give you the kind of perspective you need to accomplish this." From my experience in heaven, I now understood that Christians must use their spiritual eyes to view things from heaven's point of view, not earth's. We are also to see spiritual warfare from heaven looking down instead of from earth looking up.

Pondering Jesus' words, I wondered, "Why up above? I mean, the kingdom is in us and around us. The spirit realm is around us." As soon as that thought came, the answer from the Lord rose up in my spirit: "The kingdom rule is inside of you, but the kingdom throne is above you." Then Jesus quoted John 3:31 to me: "He who comes from above is above all; he who is of the earth is earthly and speaks of the earth. He who comes from heaven is above all."

The Lord continued, "Looking from earth's perspective is purely physical, and [that perspective] is susceptible to a consciousness of sin. Heaven's perspective is one of righteousness." I understood this to mean the spiritual eyes of the new creation are free from guilt and condemnation. When we look down from heaven, it is with spiritual authority, not worry and guilt.

I recognized Jesus' words as being a deeper expression and explanation of Hebrews 10:1–2, 22:

> For the law, having a shadow of the good things to come, and not the very image of the things, can never with these same sacrifices, which they offer continually year by year, make those who approach perfect. For then would they not have ceased to be offered? For the worshipers, once purified, would have had no more consciousness of sins....Let us draw near with a true heart in full assurance of faith, having our hearts sprinkled from an evil conscience and our bodies washed with pure water.

Jesus went on to say: "When Paul was caught up to the third heaven, he had to learn how to apply what he saw in the spirit to his earthly life. Satan buffeted Paul in an attempt to steal that revelation from him, and that's when he asked Me to remove the buffeting. But then he was able to see grace from heaven's point of view and to walk in spiritual authority. My grace is sufficient."

Verses from Paul's letter to the Ephesians exploded inside my mind. I also remembered the account in 2 Corinthians 12 where Paul talked about his abundant revelations, his thorn in the flesh, and God's sufficient grace. Everything became crystal clear as Jesus explained authority, perspective, and grace.

After the Lord finished speaking, one of the angels motioned for me to follow him. He led me through what appeared to be a wall in the throne room. There was no door. This entire room was made up of colors, sounds, and glory that were slightly different from what I experienced in the throne room. I instinctively understood that these represented different anointings required to facilitate different purposes, both on earth and in heaven. It felt as if there were innumerable rooms and anointings for every major purpose of the body of Christ on earth.

Then, just like that, the experience ended. As suddenly as I was caught up, I was brought back into the natural realm, where I found myself still sitting on the floor of the penthouse suite, praying in my spiritual language. I glanced around the room to see if anyone was watching, but since I had not moved in the physical, no one seemed to notice. I had been caught up in the spirit to the third heaven for the Lord to give me an assignment. With words straight from the lips of Jesus, this commission to teach third-heaven authority has been my priority. I have been teaching it and will continue to do so until I am instructed otherwise. I must be obedient to my heavenly assignment.

It's important for me to note that I'm not the only one commissioned to do this. Jesus impressed upon me that there were many others who would be teaching this message also. Because the church is entering an increasingly intense time before the return of Christ, it's imperative for believers to fully grasp and walk in the spiritual authority that is ours.

While contemplating my encounter, I remembered what the apostle Paul experienced in 2 Corinthians 12:1–4 (emphasis added):

> It is doubtless not profitable for me to boast. I will come to visions and revelations of the Lord: I know a man in Christ who fourteen years ago—whether in the body I do not know, or whether out of the body I do not know, God knows—such a one was

caught up to *the third heaven*. And I know such a man—whether in the body or out of the body I do not know, God knows—how he was caught up *into Paradise* and heard inexpressible words, which it is not lawful for a man to utter.

IT'S ALL ABOUT PERSPECTIVE

As I reflect on my experience, I am so humbled and thankful that the Lord considered me worthy of such an assignment. I fall short in so many ways, but He remains faithful. God is allowing me to see how the spiritual realm has been opening in the last decade. He needs people who will not be deceived but who will understand who they are in Christ, who Christ is in them, and what it means to be a new creation in Him. Born-again believers have the power of the Holy Spirit within them, and to triumph in these last days they must live from the inside out.

You too have an assignment that the Lord wants you to accomplish. He wants you to partner with Him in these last days. You will never find ultimate peace and fulfillment until you are walking in that assignment. As we move into the end of the church age and anticipate the Lord's return, it is critical that Christians learn to see things not from an earthly perspective but from their position seated with Christ in heavenly places. This heavenly perspective will empower them to move forward in every dimension of life and fulfill their individual assignments in the kingdom.

By going up and over situations in the spirit instead of dealing with them on a linear level, we as the body of Christ can accomplish so much more. We'll be able to discern the enemy's plots and plans and to exercise our dominion more effectively. No matter what situation we may be facing personally or collectively, we can experience supernatural victory if we will learn to use our authority from heaven's perspective.

Throughout this book I will be sharing some important keys that will help you better understand third-heaven authority and how to walk in the realm of dominion that Christ purchased for you. By learning how to pray effectively, develop a third-heaven mindset, access third-heaven authority, and much more, you will be equipped to handle spiritual battles and overcome obstacles that stand in the way of God's plan. Third-heaven authority belongs to you in Christ, and it is my honor to teach you what the Lord has so graciously taught me.

CHAPTER 2

A VIEW FROM HEAVEN

AFTER MY ENCOUNTER with Jesus in the third heaven, my whole life shifted in a dynamic way. I now had a mandate to teach third-heaven authority. Driven by my new calling, I began to diligently search the Scriptures for truth regarding third-heaven authority, perspective, and position.

The first passage the Holy Spirit had me zero in on was 2 Corinthians 12:1–4, which I shared in the previous chapter. In these verses, Paul notes that he had experienced visions and revelations of the Lord; then he shares a specific encounter when he was "caught up to the third heaven" and "caught up into Paradise." When Paul refers to the third heaven, it is my understanding that he is not speaking of the physical atmosphere.

Amos 9:6 states, "He who builds His layers in the sky, and has founded His strata in the earth; who calls for the waters of the sea, and pours them out on the face of the earth—the LORD is His name." This verse clearly indicates that God has built layers, strata, and palaces in the sky. But there is more than what meets the eye. Just as there are layers of the physical atmosphere, there are other-dimensional spiritual layers as well, a hierarchy of the heavens. What an amazing God, who created the heavens in such a magnificent way that it constitutes layers of both the physical and spiritual atmospheres above the earth!

From my study of the Scriptures, I've come to conclude

13

that the first heaven is the stellar heavens—what we see with our physical eyes and all that science describes. It is both the natural atmosphere containing the clouds, as well as the sun, moon, stars, planets, and galaxies. The second heaven is the spiritual atmosphere around the created heavens. As spiritual and physical beings, we exist in both realms simultaneously. The second heaven is where spiritual activity takes place, the work of both angels and demons. It is the realm of principalities and powers and is where spiritual warfare takes place.

The third heaven is the spiritual layer above the other two heavens. This is the highest realm in both location and authority. Deuteronomy 10:14 states, "Indeed, heaven and the highest heavens belong to the LORD your God, also the earth with all that is in it" (MEV). This highest realm of heaven is the residency of God, the place where His throne is located. When we refer to heaven as the eternal home of the saints, we are describing the third heaven. The third heaven is also where Jesus ascended after His resurrection. Ephesians 4:10 says, "He who descended is also He who ascended far above all the heavens that He might fill all things" (MEV).

In the context of spiritual authority, it's important to understand the Bible teaches that Jesus "ascended far above all." He was lifted up far above all—this includes everything under the earth, everything on the earth, everything in the physical first heaven, and everything in the spiritual second heaven. Third-heaven authority originates from this position of being seated above all with Christ in heavenly places. It relates to our perspective—how we look at situations and respond to them from our new nature in Christ.

When Jesus began to explain to me the importance of third-heaven authority, He said, "Learn to use your spiritual eyes to view things from heaven's point of view, not earth's point of view." This is a perspective that only the Holy Spirit can give us. It is critical, then, to rely on the help of the Holy Spirit as we study the topic of authority from the Scriptures.

THE POSITION OF THIRD-HEAVEN AUTHORITY

Most believers today have a limited understanding of their spiritual authority because they are operating in what I call linear authority. That is thinking on a linear, horizontal level when exercising spiritual authority. When we pray for others from this perspective, we often see results simply because we are being obedient to take authority over the devil as Jesus instructed us to do. But there is a higher level of authority.

In Luke 10, for example, Jesus commissioned the seventy disciples to go into every city and announce the coming of God's kingdom. After fulfilling their assignment, the disciples returned to Jesus rejoicing that the devils were subject to His name. In response to their excitement Jesus said, "Behold, I give you the authority to trample on serpents and scorpions, and over all the power of the enemy" (Luke 10:19). Here, Jesus was revealing to His disciples the magnificent authority His name carried and how it could manifest when they were ministering to others.

I have seen God graciously do incredible things through me as I walked in this linear type of authority. I've seen numerous people born again, healed, and set free.

If someone asks for prayer, I simply lay hands on them, and they recover. Whenever I'm obedient to take authority over the enemy in a person's life as Jesus instructed His disciples to do, powerful results follow.

Third-heaven authority operates by the same principle. However, it is an enhanced, higher view of the supreme power we have in Christ. It can be described as having a perspective of looking down from the higher heavenly position to the lower spiritual and earthly levels. It is exercising authority from Jesus' position in heaven as He is seated above all. This authority flows from a revelation of the ultimate authority Jesus carries and that we are positioned in Him through the new birth.

As I began to understand the weightiness of Jesus' supreme position above all, I launched a deeper study into scriptures regarding this topic. Here are just some of the passages that declare His position above all.

> Be exalted, O God, *above* the heavens; let Your glory
> be *above all* the earth.
> —PSALM 57:5, EMPHASIS ADDED

> For You, O LORD, are Most High *above all* the earth;
> You are exalted far *above all* gods.
> —PSALM 97:9, MEV, EMPHASIS ADDED

> He who comes from *above* is *above all*. He who is of
> the earth is earthly and speaks of the earth. He who
> comes from heaven is *above all*.
> —JOHN 3:31, MEV, EMPHASIS ADDED

> Which He worked in Christ when He raised Him
> from the dead and seated Him at His right hand in

the heavenly places, far *above all* principality and
power and might and dominion, and every name
that is named, not only in this age but also in that
which is to come.
—EPHESIANS 1:20–21, EMPHASIS ADDED

One God and Father of all, who is *above all*, and
through all, and in you all.
—EPHESIANS 4:6, MEV, EMPHASIS ADDED

If then you were raised with Christ, seek those
things which are *above*, where Christ is, sitting at
the right hand of God. Set your mind on things
above, not on things on the earth.
—COLOSSIANS 3:1–2, EMPHASIS ADDED

Every good gift and every perfect gift is from *above*,
and comes down from the Father of lights, with
whom there is no variation or shadow of turning.
—JAMES 1:17, EMPHASIS ADDED

But the wisdom that is from *above* is first pure, then
peaceable, gentle, willing to yield, full of mercy
and good fruits, without partiality and without
hypocrisy.
—JAMES 3:17, EMPHASIS ADDED

These passages clearly reveal the powerful truth of
Christ's exalted position. He is seated above all, ruling and
reigning from a place of supreme authority, power, might,
and dominion. There is no power greater. No name can
be exalted or elevated above His. No situation or demonic
force is greater than He is. Everything is underneath Him,
for He is truly above all!

And here's some more really good news. Because of Christ's exalted position and supreme authority, everything that we have in Him is also above all. "If then you were raised with Christ, seek those things which are *above*, where Christ is, sitting at the right hand of God" (Col. 3:1, emphasis added). Just as Christ is exalted above all, so are we! We are sitting right next to Him.

Ephesians 2:6 makes it clear that as believers God has "raised us up together, and made us sit together in the heavenly places in Christ Jesus." Now, as raised-up children of God, we are to go through life with an "above all" mindset. This is the wonder of the new creation, a life that can now reign above all as we learn to walk in the full character of the One that empowers us.

To help me understand the greater dimension of His authority, Jesus allowed me to be taken to the third heaven so I could impart that revelation to others. However, you don't have to personally experience a vision of the third heaven to know the fullness of Jesus' power and authority. You already have the written Word of God. It contains everything you need to know regarding the truth of Jesus' completed work and the scope of His power. You also have the Holy Spirit inside you to guide and illuminate as you walk out this revelation. God's Word and the Holy Spirit have already equipped you to understand third-heaven authority.

Once you begin to grasp how your position relates to spiritual authority, you can operate on a much higher plane in the Spirit and see greater results in prayer. I can testify that understanding authority from this perspective has wonderfully enhanced the effectiveness of my prayer life and ministry.

TWO REALMS OF EXISTENCE

Another key to operating in third-heaven authority is understanding the difference between the spiritual and physical realms. What we see and hear on this earth are all part of the physical, natural realm. The spiritual realm, however, is made of what we can't see—heaven, Jesus, the Holy Spirit, angels, demons, and so on. Of the two realms, the spiritual is always greater than the physical. Although we can't see the spiritual realm with our natural eyes, the activity in the spirit produces what occurs in the physical realm.

God's kingdom in the spirit is the parent of His kingdom on the earth. The Bible teaches us that "God is Spirit, and those who worship Him must worship Him in spirit and truth" (John 4:24, MEV). God, who is a spiritual being, created the physical universe, Hebrews 11:3 expounds on this: "By faith we understand that the worlds were framed by the word of God, so that the things which are seen were not made of things which are visible." In other words, God created both the spiritual and physical realms, and it is the spiritual realities that give life to the natural world.

When God created man, He uniquely designed him to exist in both worlds simultaneously through His three-part nature of spirit, soul, and body. We see evidence of the existence of man's triune being in 1 Thessalonians 5:23: "Now may the God of peace Himself sanctify you completely; and may your whole spirit, soul, and body be preserved blameless at the coming of our Lord Jesus Christ." This scripture reveals the inner and outward parts of man working together to create the full picture of who we are and how we connect to both the physical and spiritual worlds.

The physical body is the part of your being that relates to the earthly realm. It is the visible part of you that runs, plays, works, sleeps, and eats. When people first meet you, it is this outward part of you they see and know. People may describe you by your physical characteristics such as hair color, eye color, height, voice, and facial expressions. Yet while your physical body is the visible part of your identity, it serves to house the part of you that people don't see. This inner man is your spirit, and it was created to relate to, engage with, and participate in the spiritual realm. Your spirit is the real you, and it is the part of your being that comes alive unto God at salvation. Inside your spirit is where the Holy Spirit lives, and it is also your spirit that fellowships with God.

As important as our physical bodies are, they are subjected to our spirits. Your body was formed from the earth, but it's kept alive by your spirit man inside you. Genesis 2:7 says, "Then the LORD God formed man from the dust of the ground and breathed into his nostrils the breath of life, and man became a living being" (MEV). It is with the spirit man that we contact God and operate in the spiritual realm.

The bridge between the body and spirit that keeps these two working together is the part of us called the soul. This is what constitutes the mind, will, and emotions. The soul can operate from the knowledge we perceive in our spirits by the Holy Spirit. At the same time, it can also process knowledge that comes to us through our five physical senses of seeing, touching, hearing, smelling, and tasting.

It's important to understand that God created us to

operate in both the spiritual and natural realms simultaneously. These two worlds coexist around us. We are not merely human beings who are having a spiritual experience; we are spiritual beings having a human experience. This ability to function in both realms at the same time is key to understanding how third-heaven authority works.

Within the spiritual and physical realms are unique dimensions, realities, dynamics, and authority. In the natural realm there are the dimensions of time, space, and matter that don't exist in the spiritual realm. The spiritual realm, on the other hand, operates by faith, a spiritual force that is a product of God's realm. It is not governed by sight, which is a product of the physical realm.

If you have received Jesus Christ as your Lord and Savior, then you were created to operate in the realm of the Spirit. You are a new creation in Christ. The Holy Spirit lives inside you and communicates with you. You are a third-heaven creation operating in third-heaven revelation with the capability of functioning in third-heaven authority. It is your right as a son or daughter of the One exalted above all.

My prayer is that the eyes of your spirit will be opened to the great treasure of authority placed inside you by the Holy Spirit. May you begin to hear His voice more clearly than ever before. I pray for visions, dreams, revelation, and angelic encounters to increase in your life. Most importantly, I pray that your spirit will be enlightened by the truth of God's Word as the Holy Spirit brings fresh insight and revelation.

As you pursue a greater understanding of third-heaven authority, I believe the Holy Spirit will enlighten your heart to the reality of Jesus' authority as supreme and above all. From that position of being seated with Him in heavenly places, you'll be able to see everything around you from a brand-new perspective: You are not located below circumstances, but above them!

When the revelation of third-heaven authority takes root in your heart, it will change the way you pray about situations and minister to others. Your awareness of the spiritual realm will increase as you learn to operate in the Spirit while living on the earth. God has purposefully created you to oppose and conquer the works of darkness through the mighty, all-surpassing power and authority of Jesus Christ.

CHAPTER 3

THE THIRD-HEAVEN EPISTLE

IT WAS DURING my heavenly encounter that I realized how closely Paul's letter to the Ephesians matched the perspective and revelations I had received. Following my experience, the more I read his letter, the more I was personally convinced that the book to the church at Ephesus was really Paul's third-heaven epistle. I'll explain.

To operate properly in third-heaven authority, it is imperative that we have a clear understanding of our identity in Christ. While we hear it talked about a lot these days, it's almost mind-boggling how many Christians really don't grasp who they are and what they have access to as God's kids. Because of this, they are, as Paul says, "children, tossed to and fro and carried about with every wind of doctrine, by the trickery of men, in the cunning craftiness of deceitful plotting" (Eph. 4:14). They're definitely not walking in third-heaven authority.

Knowing and embracing our identity as believers is the critical first step to walking in the full favor and power that is rightfully ours. While the truth of our identity in Christ is woven throughout the New Testament, the Book of Ephesians gives us a laser-focused emphasis on it. In this chapter I'd like to take a closer look at Ephesians and show how our identity in Christ applies to third-heaven authority.

As I shared in chapter 1, the passage that came to my heart after my visit to the third heaven was 2 Corinthians

12:1–4, where Paul described a similar spiritual experience. Although Paul says this happened to "a man in Christ," I believe he was speaking of himself when he wrote:

> It is doubtless not profitable for me to boast. I will come to visions and revelations of the Lord: I know a man in Christ who fourteen years ago—whether in the body I do not know, or whether out of the body I do not know, God knows—such a one was caught up to the third heaven. And I know such a man—whether in the body or out of the body I do not know, God knows—how he was caught up into Paradise and heard inexpressible words, which it is not lawful for a man to utter.

In describing the vision, Paul used the phrase "caught up to the third heaven." During this catching-up moment, he caught a glimpse into spiritual realities from a unique vantage point. After undoubtedly seeing amazing other-dimensional realities and hearing words that were "inexpressible," Paul now had a broader perspective of the operations of the spirit realm. It is my personal opinion that Paul didn't go public with what he'd seen or heard immediately. Instead, he took some time to process everything. Before sharing with others, he had to come to an understanding of what the Spirit was teaching him through the experience. Since the Book of Ephesians was written about five years after the second letter to the Corinthians, it seems to me that God had Paul in a season of waiting and learning before releasing him to teach the elements of that revelation.

It's reasonable to think that once Paul received permission to share the vision and the truth he'd gleaned from the Spirit concerning it, he began writing the Book of Ephesians. The reason I believe this is that Ephesians contains the powerful revelation of the believer's identity in Christ and all that it encompasses. Moreover, Paul consistently used the word *above* in his writing in Ephesians, which makes perfect sense coming from his new third-heaven vantage point.

In addition to the word *above*, the Book of Ephesians contains twenty-five verses that include phrases such as "in Him," "in whom," "in the Beloved," "with [or in or by] Christ," and "through Him." Thirteen of those verses are found in Ephesians 1, nine in Ephesians 2, and three in Ephesians 3, and they all relate to specific attributes of the believer's life in Christ. Overall, Ephesians is a book that delves into the deeper realms of spiritual authority. A magnificent epistle, it is full of powerful nuggets and gems regarding the believer's conquering position, identity, and inheritance that are all anchored in the finished work of the resurrected Christ.

THE TREASURY OF EPHESIANS

Some of those nuggets and gems are obvious, while others must be mined. We will examine both, but in this chapter I'd like us to do a little digging. Together, let's unearth some key verses that reveal various aspects of our spiritual authority with regard to "heavenly places." You'll love these gemstones of truth. They changed my life, and I'm sure they will yours too!

Throughout Ephesians' six chapters, Paul uses the term "heavenly places" in reference to our spiritual position. This is a connection to viewing things from the position of "above," or the third heaven, where Jesus is seated, ruling, and reigning. It's terminology that points to who we are in Christ.

Ephesians 1:3 says, "Blessed be the God and Father of our Lord Jesus Christ, who has blessed us with every spiritual blessing in the *heavenly places* in Christ" (MEV, emphasis added). Ephesians 1:19–20 goes on to say, "And what is the exceeding greatness of His power toward us who believe, according to the working of His mighty power which He worked in Christ when He raised Him from the dead and seated Him at His right hand in the *heavenly places*" (emphasis added). As we saw in the previous chapter, Ephesians 2:6 states that God "raised us up together, and made us sit together in the *heavenly places* in Christ Jesus" (emphasis added).

Paul also uses the term *heavenly places* in reference to the spiritual activity going on above and around us. This can be ascribed to the location of the second heaven that I mentioned earlier. From our vantage point on the earth, the second heaven is situated above and around us but below the third heaven, where Christ is seated. Again, this cosmic in-between region is where spiritual warfare takes place.

We can see that there are angelic beings in the heavenlies in Ephesians 3:10: "So that now the manifold wisdom of God might be made known by the church to the principalities and powers *in the heavenly places*" (MEV, emphasis added). As Paul wraps up the epistle with a grand exposé on spiritual warfare in the sixth chapter, he again refers to demonic powers in the second heaven as well: "For we do not wrestle against flesh and blood, but against principalities, against powers, against the rulers of the darkness of this age, against spiritual hosts of wickedness *in the heavenly places*" (Eph. 6:12, emphasis added).

Although spiritual warfare takes place in the heavenlies, it is subjugated to the authority of the highest heavenly place: the throne room of heaven. It is from his revelation of the third heaven that Paul wrote to help us understand how spiritual battles are fought and won. Because of our position of being raised up and seated with Christ in heavenly places, we have the advantage of being far above all.

As you can see, a major aspect of third-heaven authority is understanding who we are in the Lord Jesus Christ. This is critical because the darkness around us is no joke. It is very real. The enemy is hell-bent on taking us out. He's a thief and a liar that is focused solely on stealing, killing, and destroying the world and God's people. He wants us bound and enslaved in all sorts of sin, strongholds, and false attachments. As believers, however, there is no need for intimidation because we are called to walk in authority over Satan and his demonic system.

Yet if we are to do so, we must understand what Jesus conquered in His death, burial, and resurrection. We also need to recognize that in the new birth, we have been made alive unto God. Sin no longer has reign over our bodies. Instead, we can live victoriously over the lust of the flesh from that place of being risen in Christ. Anytime we exercise authority over the evil one, we can do so without fear, intimidation, or defeat because Jesus has already triumphed over him. We've been seated with Christ in heavenly places and have been granted high-level authority, thanks to all Christ has wrought through His resurrection. How exciting and powerful!

PRAYING FROM THE HEAVENLY PLACE OF AUTHORITY

Now that we've uncovered this first major gemstone from Ephesians, I want to demonstrate how this revelation can help you pray more effectively. Who doesn't want more impactful prayers? Although the Lord graciously granted me an uncommon supernatural experience to help me understand authority as it relates to spiritual warfare, visions are not necessarily required to understand the dynamics of third-heaven authority. What is necessary is for the written Word of God to be so ingrained in us that it becomes a natural part of us. The Word of God is the final authority for the believer, and we have to know it well. The Word of God is written for every single believer and is understood as the Holy Spirit brings illumination to our minds.

If you desire to increase your understanding of spiritual authority, I encourage you to dig deep into the Book of Ephesians. Look for every verse that includes the phrases "in Christ," "in Him," "in the Beloved," "in the Lord," "in Whom," "by Christ," "from Whom," "through Christ," and "with Christ." Highlight those verses in your Bible and write them out in your journal or on note cards. Study them daily, meditate on them, and pray them over yourself. Ask the Holy Spirit to enlighten your eyes to the truth of God's Word and to everything Christ has purchased for you.

As you take time to study Ephesians, the Holy Spirit will begin to reveal to you the power of the resurrection, Jesus' triumph over sin, the reality of the new birth, and your inheritance in Christ. You'll also discover keys to overcoming the works of darkness and what it means to fight in the Spirit clothed in the full armor of God. The Holy Spirit will bring revelation to your heart regarding your position in Christ and the victory you have in Him. You'll begin to understand the dynamics of spiritual warfare and how to fight in the spirit from the place of being risen and seated with Christ above all. Everything you need to know is right there in the wonderful Word of God!

When it comes to prayer, the revelation of being seated with Christ in heavenly places greatly enhances our effectiveness in exercising our authority over the works of darkness. We don't pray from a position of being under the circumstances, but rather from a vantage point of being above them as Christ is above them. This is an advantageous position of prayer, for it's from this position that we are able to see the bigger picture, the strategies of the enemy, and the ruling authority we've been given in Christ.

If we'll yield to Him in prayer, the Holy Spirit will show us exactly how to pray over every situation. He will lead us into truth based on the Word of God because, as Jesus said, He is "the Spirit of truth" (John 14:17). The Bible also teaches that the Holy Spirit is our Helper: "But when the Helper comes, whom I shall send to you from the Father, the Spirit of truth who proceeds from the Father, He will testify of Me" (John 15:26).

The same description is found in John 14: "And I will pray the Father, and He will give you another Helper, that He may abide with you forever—the Spirit of truth, whom the world cannot receive, because it neither sees Him nor knows Him; but you know Him, for He dwells with you and will be in you" (vv. 16–17). The word translated

"Helper" in this passage is the Greek term *paraklētos*, which is used to refer to "one who pleads another's cause... an intercessor."[1] So anytime we need help in prayer, we can ask the Holy Spirit to aid us in our weakness, and He will teach us, lead us, and guide us in our times of prayer.

Most often, the Holy Spirit will lead us to a specific scripture that relates to the issue we are covering in prayer. He'll then give us revelation regarding how to apply that verse in prayer to the situation at hand. By leading us to pray in line with Scripture, the Holy Spirit is acting as our helper in prayer. He is enlightening our understanding to the verse or passage and showing us how to deal a death blow to the enemy by using the power of God's Word. This is part of the armor mentioned in Ephesians 6:17: "Take the helmet of salvation and the sword of the Spirit, which is the word of God" (MEV).

Another way the Holy Spirit will help us in our times of prayer is by revealing the strategies and tactics of the enemy. In 1 Peter 5:8–9 the Bible admonishes us, "Be sober, be vigilant; because your adversary the devil walks about like a roaring lion, seeking whom he may devour. Resist him, steadfast in the faith, knowing that the same sufferings are experienced by your brotherhood in the world." Paul writes in 2 Corinthians 2:11 that we should not be ignorant of the devil's devices. Ephesians 6:11 instructs us that we are to put on the whole armor of God in order to stand against the wiles of the devil.

In reality, the Holy Spirit is our secret weapon in spiritual warfare. A few years ago my wife, CK, and her friend Kathie Walters went on a sightseeing/ministry trip to the United Kingdom with a group. About a week into their trip, I began to feel that something wasn't right, and I began to intercede for them in my heavenly prayer language. (We'll talk more about the power of praying in tongues in later chapters.) Suddenly the Holy Spirit took me up into the atmosphere directly over the hotel where they were staying. From there I saw that evil spirits of anger and strife had infiltrated the group. It was a demonic strategy manifesting through a few individuals. The devil intended to shut down the move of the Holy Spirit by the resulting chaos and confusion. The discord was strange and out of place on a trip of that sort.

When I saw the enemy's tactic, I immediately took authority over it in the name of Jesus. Then I released peace and deliverance over the whole group. The next day my wife and I spoke on the phone, and I shared my prayer experience with her. She confirmed that they had indeed been dealing with a situation of anger and strife with a couple of people, and it was affecting everyone. There was no way I could have known this was happening on the other side of the world except by the Holy Spirit. As a result of the discernment He brought, that spirit's power was broken. This is an example of being lifted above a situation and having a victorious outcome through the Lord Jesus Christ.

There are so many situations in our lives that will change if we take them before the Lord in prayer from the vantage point of being seated with Christ "above all." By understanding our high position in Christ, we can exercise our authority over the devil and all the works of darkness. We can bind, loose, and release the power of the kingdom—all from that elevated place.

Praying Paul's Prayers

As you are digging into and meditating on the Book of Ephesians, ask the Holy Spirit to enlighten your understanding of the wonders of your inheritance in Christ and the position of authority you have in Him. Also, I admonish you to take certain passages that Paul prayed over the church and pray them over yourself and your fellow believers. You can make them personal by replacing the pronouns with *I, me,* or *my.* If you're praying these over a friend, insert his or her name into the passage as you lift that person up before the Lord.

There are two specific passages in Ephesians I encourage you to include in your daily prayer time. The first one is Ephesians 1:17–23, which I have already converted into a prayer:

> [I pray] that the God of our Lord Jesus Christ, the Father of glory, may give to [me] the spirit of wisdom and revelation in the knowledge of Him, the eyes of [my] understanding being enlightened; that [I] may know what is the hope of His calling, what are the riches of the glory of His inheritance in the saints, and what is the exceeding greatness of His power toward [me] who believe[s], according to the working of His mighty power which He worked in Christ when He raised Him from the dead and seated Him at His right hand in the heavenly places, far above all principality and power and might and dominion, and every name that is named, not only in this age but also in that which is to come. And He put all things under His feet, and gave Him to

be head over all things to the church, which is His body, the fullness of Him who fills all in all.

The second passage is Ephesians 3:14–21, which I also adapted into a prayer here:

For this reason I bow my knees to the Father of our Lord Jesus Christ, from whom the whole family in heaven and earth is named, that He would grant [me], according to the riches of His glory, to be strengthened with might through His Spirit in the inner man, that Christ may dwell in [my heart] through faith; that [I], being rooted and grounded in love, may be able to comprehend with all the saints what is the width and length and depth and height— to know the love of Christ which passes knowledge; that [I] may be filled with all the fullness of God. Now to Him who is able to do exceedingly abundantly above all that [I] ask or think, according to the power that works in [me], to Him be glory in the church by Christ Jesus to all generations, forever and ever. Amen.

As you pray these prayers, listen to them in your heart. The revelation of Christ's power and your inheritance is not something that God is keeping a secret from you. It is something He longs to reveal to you by His Word and through His Spirit. It's a revelation He has for you because you are part of the family of God. You've been bought with a price—the precious blood of Jesus— and your position of authority is part of the inheritance of your salvation.

You don't have to be defined by the circumstances surrounding you. By the power of Jesus, you can rise above every situation. Deliverance and healing are yours. Salvation belongs to you and your family. You can experience financial health. Your marriage can be blessed. Your children don't have to live in rebellion. Depression doesn't have to control your emotions. You can have a full life in the joy of the Lord, all because you've been risen with Christ and seated with Him above all.

Of course, problems will arise from time to time. That's life in a fallen world, and we have to deal with the flesh and the devil. The Bible tells us that we will have trials and tribulations in life. However, Jesus encouraged us to be of good cheer because He has overcome the world (John 16:33).

One way Jesus empowered us to overcome the world is by enabling us to overcome the perspective of the world. A believer who is not aware of his position in Christ is still trapped in the world's viewpoint of defeat, sickness, lack, sin, and brokenness. This attitude locks people into small-mindedness and the normal grind of earthly living. This is why it's so important for our minds to be renewed daily by God's Word. Romans 12:2 tells us, "Do not be conformed to this world, but be transformed by the renewing of your mind, that you may prove what is the good and acceptable and perfect will of God." What's interesting about this verse is that conforming to the world is a natural process that takes no effort. But transformation is a supernatural act.

Something supernatural happens when we renew our minds to the truth. God supernaturally transforms us— that's a promise! You can come into God's presence and pray, "God, You promised that when I renew my mind to Your truth, You will transform me." Then begin declaring what God's Word says about who you are. (See the appendix for several verses to get you started.) If you do that, God promises you will come out of that place realigned to Him in accordance with your position.

The more we meditate on the Word, the more our minds are changed from low-level earthly thinking to God's high-level thinking. We begin to see things from heaven's vantage point and not just from an earthly view. That is why it's so important for us to read the Bible daily and pray in the Holy Spirit. These two things alone will shift our entire outlook on life and how we approach our daily responsibilities. The earthly mindset and perspective will grow dimmer and dimmer as we rise higher and higher in our understanding of our position in Christ.

As Paul the apostle prayed in Ephesians 1:17–23, I pray also for you.

> I pray "that the God of our Lord Jesus Christ, the Father of glory, may give to you the spirit of wisdom and revelation in the knowledge of Him, the eyes of your understanding being enlightened; that you may know what is the hope of His calling, what are the riches of the glory of His inheritance in [you], and what is the exceeding greatness of His power toward [you] who believe[s], according to the working of His mighty power which He worked in Christ when He raised Him from the dead and seated Him at His right hand in the heavenly places, far above all principality and power and might and dominion, and every name that is named, not only in this age but also in that which is

*to come. And He put all things under His feet,
and gave Him to be head over all things to the
church, which is His body, the fullness of Him
who fills all in all." Amen.*

As you press in to God, I pray the Lord will reveal the higher dimensions of the spirit to you. May you begin to flow in greater revelation than you've experienced up to now. I pray the Holy Spirit will teach you how to move in His gifts, even in your own prayer time. May visions and dreams from the Holy Spirit increase in your life.

As you fill your mind and being with God's Word and take to heart the truths in Ephesians written from Paul's "above all" view, you will experience greater spiritual victories. May you see the things of this world from your position of being raised and seated with Christ in the heavenly places.

CHAPTER 4

AUTHORITY ON EARTH AS IN HEAVEN

To WALK IN third-heaven authority, it is vital that we learn to discern the flow of God's power and tap into it. When we do, our prayers become ignited. Much like a boat that follows the current of a river doesn't have to fight against the waves, when we follow the flow of God's power, we won't find ourselves struggling in our own strength to bring about what God has for us or, worse, going against what God is doing.

In the kingdom of God, spiritual authority flows from heaven, where Christ is seated far above all principality and power, down to us on earth below. It's much like the flow of power in the military. Orders come from the top down. Imagine if you were a military leader and had direct access to the commander in chief. Better yet, imagine if the one at the top, the one with the most power, authorized you to carry his same top-down authority. Imagine how much easier it would be to accomplish your mission. We have that authorization from the supreme commander in chief of the universe! Christ has given us His authority from above in the heavenly place, where we are seated right next to Him, and it flows down from the realm of the spirit through us to the realm of the natural.

First Peter 1:3–5 is a great verification of this:

> Blessed be the God and Father of our Lord Jesus
> Christ, who according to His abundant mercy has

> begotten us again to a living hope through the res-
> urrection of Jesus Christ from the dead, to an inher-
> itance incorruptible and undefiled and that does not
> fade away, reserved in heaven for you, who are kept
> by the power of God through faith for salvation
> ready to be revealed in the last time.

The passage tells us that through Jesus' resurrection we are given an inheritance in heaven, where we are seated with Christ, that is "kept by the power of God through faith." Faith is a key here. Remember, God exists outside of time. So does the eternal realm. What is future to us is the present with God. Thus, we are seated with Christ now and have His authority now. By faith we see it and apply it to our current realities.

The spiritual realm is the parent to the natural realm. Everything first takes place in the unseen realm of the spirit, which eventually gives birth to the things that are visible in the physical realm. When we take our authority in the spirit, we will ultimately see the effects in the natural.

This flow of authority from heaven above to earth below and from the spirit realm to the natural realm is revealed in Jesus' teaching on prayer in Matthew 6. Often referred to as the Lord's Prayer, this familiar passage begins: "Our Father who is in heaven, hallowed be Your name. Your kingdom come; Your will be done on earth, as it is in heaven" (vv. 9–10, MEV). In this simple but profound teaching on prayer, Jesus conveys the source and proper flow of authority—from heaven to earth and from the unseen spiritual realm to the natural realm.

Tapping into this flow of authority that is rightfully

ours will ignite prayers like the flow of electricity through jumper cables sparks an engine, or the forceful flow of waters rushing through a dam generates electrical power to light up a city. Whether you are praying for yourself, your family, your friends, your city, or your nation, your prayers can change environments and situations when you tap the Source in the spirit where transformation is released. Going back to the analogy of the boat on the river, our job is to find out where the Holy Spirit is flowing and jump in.

Exercising this authority is certainly critical now, but it's going to become even more so as we move into the future. In the days to come, those who take full advantage of their God-given authority to wage spiritual warfare will be the ones who trample the enemy and live in victory. Before Christ's return, the activity in the second heaven will increase greatly. There will be heightened actions on both sides. The devil's kingdom will be hard at work bringing darkness, despair, and deception while God's kingdom simultaneously will be manifesting light and glory. Demonic activity will increase, but so will angelic activity.

Even now we are seeing both light and darkness at work all across the world. Thousands of years ago, Isaiah prophesied about this time in history.

> For behold, the darkness shall cover the earth, and deep darkness the people; but the LORD will arise over you, and His glory will be seen upon you. The Gentiles shall come to your light, and kings to the brightness of your rising.
>
> —ISAIAH 60:2–3

In recent years there has been an increase in spiritual activity in both the kingdom of light and the kingdom of darkness. Because we are entering a new era in the church, understanding our authority in Christ and how it operates is essential to the work of the kingdom and the advancement of the gospel.

THE AUTHORITY IN THE NAME OF JESUS

There is power in the name of Jesus. We may have heard that preached from pulpits and sung in worship songs since childhood. The question is, Do we really believe it? More important, Do we walk in that reality? Many will say there is power in Jesus' name, yet they live as though Jesus never rose from the dead. Recognizing the power in Jesus' name is key in understanding the flow of authority. But before we can utilize the power of His name, we must believe Jesus is real, alive, and fully present!

Paul said in 1 Corinthians 15 that if Christ is not risen, then we are still in our sins, our faith is in vain, and we are to be pitied among men. On top of that, we would be calling Paul, the disciples, and more than five hundred others false witnesses because they all claimed to have seen the risen Jesus (v. 6). In other words, if Christ didn't rise from the dead, Paul and the other disciples were liars of the worst kind. "But," Paul said, "Christ has indeed been raised from the dead" (v. 20, NIV).

Peter affirmed this also. Knowing he was about to be martyred for his faith, Peter said, "For we did not follow cunningly devised fables when we made known to you the power and coming of our Lord Jesus Christ, but were eyewitnesses of His majesty" (2 Pet. 1:16). The same guy who denied Jesus three times before the rooster crowed would now rather die, even in a horrific fashion, than deny Jesus. Why? Because like Paul, he had seen the risen Jesus.

Jesus is indeed risen and is now reigning in heaven, and whenever a believer declares His name in faith over any situation, spiritual authority is immediately released and flows down through that believer. The name of Jesus enforces what the blood of Jesus has accomplished.

Right before His ascension into heaven, Jesus revealed this truth to His disciples in the Great Commission: "*In My name* they will cast out demons; they will speak with new tongues; they will take up serpents; and if they drink anything deadly, it will by no means hurt them; they will lay hands on the sick, and they will recover" (Mark 16:17–18, emphasis added). Here, Jesus was teaching His disciples how to use His name to exercise the spiritual authority they had been given as they responded to His call to "go into all the world and preach the gospel to every creature" (Mark 16:15).

Not long ago, I had an unusual vision of just how powerful the name of Jesus is when released in faith. I was in a time of prayer and had been interceding in the Holy Spirit over our ministry partners. There were several situations that had come to my attention—people were asking for prayer regarding their finances, salvation for their loved ones, physical healing, and all sorts of things. Because I was genuinely concerned for these many needs, I was seeking the power of God to flow through people's lives. It was the longing of my heart for all of them to receive their covenant provision, healing, and salvation.

While I was praying, I was instantly taken into the spiritual realm. Standing in front of me was a horrific horde of demons. At first I saw just one or two advancing toward me. Then another one appeared, and then another. The scene intensified, and soon several demons were heading in my direction!

I recognized the spiritual implication of what was happening. These demonic spirits were behind several of the challenges our partners were facing. I wasn't just praying over their natural needs; I was dealing with the unseen spiritual forces causing these particular problems.

Suddenly a sword appeared in my right hand. I lifted it and began to attack. Each time I swung the sword, I declared, "In the name of Jesus!" As I continued in this fashion, I took authority over all the supporters' issues, using the authority in the name of Jesus. For the person suffering from cancer I boldly declared, "I rebuke cancer in the name of Jesus!" For the person who was dealing with severe financial lack I prayed, "I rebuke poverty in the name of Jesus!"

From that moment on, I went through the whole list of prayer requests, exercising my authority in the spirit, declaring the name of Jesus over every problem, and rebuking the demonic force behind every issue. No longer was I overwhelmed by the barrage of demons. Instead, they were scattering everywhere as I used the name of Jesus and rebuked them in His authority.

During the battle, I noticed a strong presence behind me. I could feel it was an angel encouraging and strengthening me. It was infusing me with this understanding of how to wage warfare against the horde of advancing demons.

After I had defeated the last demon, I stood there before the Lord with my sword down in my right hand. I noticed it was dripping with blood, which is symbolic of the victory of warfare. The angel standing behind me moved next to my right hand. I saw that he was about nine feet tall and dressed in ancient armor. I remember his thick leather armor had metal joints and buckles, and he was wearing sandals on his feet. His sword was dripping with blood, just as mine was, and I realized this angel had valiantly helped me win the warfare.

A thundering voice then reverberated through the atmosphere. I heard the words, "Mike and Michael, an unbeatable team." I knew it was the Lord speaking to me and to the angel standing next to me. The voice continued, "Mike, you are created a warrior. Be the warrior."

While we can't see them with our natural eyes, powerful things are always happening in the spirit realm when we pray and use our authority in the name of Jesus. Angels are stepping onto the scene, demons are fleeing, and all kinds of enemies are being defeated. We emerge from our time of prayer as warriors in Christ because we've learned to handle well the spiritual weapons given to us. We don't shrink back from the onslaught of the enemy. Instead, we boldly confront darkness clothed with our spiritual armor and assert our authority over the devil and all his cohorts in the mighty name of Jesus.

THE NAME ABOVE EVERY NAME

The name of Jesus carries the heaviest weight in both the spiritual and natural realms. Think about this for a moment. When someone explodes with anger, you never hear them shout "Oh, Buddha!" or "Muhammad!" They always use the Lord's name. In movies and TV shows, the popular thing among unbelievers is to degrade the name of Jesus. Have you ever wondered why? It's because Satan knows Jesus is the most powerful name in the universe. At that name demons tremble, and so should we. We should have a holy fear of the power in the name of Jesus. Satan wants that name to be devalued and made common, to be trampled on, so people lose sight of how much power it holds.

Nothing in any physical or spiritual place is higher than the name of Jesus. The Bible tells us, "Therefore God also has highly exalted Him and given Him *the name which is above every name*, that at the name of Jesus every knee should bow, of those in heaven, and of those on earth, and of those under the earth" (Phil. 2:9–10, emphasis added). His name is above everything in the second and third heavens, including all the angels, created beings, rulers of darkness in high places as mentioned in Ephesians 6:12, and departed saints. The name of Jesus is above everything in the strata of space that includes the sun, moon, stars, planets, and galaxies.

When it comes to things on the earth, the name of Jesus is higher than any force of nature, including hurricanes, tornadoes, earthquakes, and other natural disasters. His name is higher than the most powerful leader or celebrity. Everything under the earth—demons, departed spirits, and all darkness—must bow down! If something has a name, it is subjugated to the highest authority of all—the powerful name of Jesus!

According to Hebrews, His name is higher than the angels':

...having become so much better than the angels, as He has by inheritance obtained *a more excellent name* than they.

—HEBREWS 1:4, EMPHASIS ADDED

When Jesus was seated at God's right hand in heavenly places, His name was exalted above everything past, present, and future, as Ephesians 1:20–21 states (emphasis added):

...which He worked in Christ when He raised Him from the dead and seated Him at His right hand in the heavenly places, *far above* all principality and power and might and dominion, and *every name that is named*, not only in this age but also in that which is to come.

THE NAME OF JESUS IN PRAYER

Praying in the weighty name of Jesus is more than tacking "in Jesus' name" to the end of a prayer before saying amen. It's about walking in the awareness and reality of God's presence, authority, and power. In His earthly ministry, Jesus taught His disciples the importance of gathering together for prayer in His name.

Again I say to you that if two of you agree on earth concerning anything that they ask, it will be done for them by My Father in heaven. For where two or three are gathered together *in My name*, I am there in the midst of them.

—MATTHEW 18:19–20, EMPHASIS ADDED

It doesn't take crowds of thousands or even hundreds for God's power to be released. Miracles can happen even when just two or three individuals agree together in His name. If you need an answer from God—wisdom, healing, financial help, direction, or anything else—you can simply call on a friend who will agree with you for your answer according to God's Word and in the name of Jesus. God's power will be released the moment you pray together in Jesus' name. His name carries that much weight when you pray!

The Bible also tells us that when we ask God for something in accordance with His Word and in the name of Jesus, our prayers will be answered.

> And whatever you ask *in My name*, that I will do, that the Father may be glorified in the Son. If you ask anything *in My name*, I will do it.
> —JOHN 14:13–14, EMPHASIS ADDED

> And in that day you will ask Me nothing. Most assuredly, I say to you, whatever you ask the Father *in My name* He will give you. Until now you have asked nothing *in My name*. Ask, and you will receive, that your joy may be full.
> —JOHN 16:23–24, EMPHASIS ADDED

Scripture makes it abundantly clear that praying in the name of Jesus is the key to answered prayer.

THE NAME OF JESUS IN THE GREAT COMMISSION

As I mentioned previously, we exercise the authority Jesus delegated to us in the Great Commission through the use of His name. As we carry out the work of the kingdom, we have heaven's power backing us up when we use the name of Jesus. This is how we exert authority in the spirit as we advance the kingdom of heaven through whatever assignment God has given us.

Let's look at the passage typically referred to as the Great Commission.

> And Jesus came and spoke to them, saying, *"All authority has been given to Me* in heaven and on earth. Go therefore and make disciples of all the nations, baptizing them in the name of the Father and of the Son and of the Holy Spirit, teaching them to observe all things that I have commanded you; and lo, I am with you always, even to the end of the age." Amen.
> —MATTHEW 28:18–20, EMPHASIS ADDED

As referenced previously, in Mark 16:17–18, Jesus adds this to His description of our commission (emphasis added):

> And these signs will follow those who believe: *In My name* they will cast out demons; they will speak with new tongues; they will take up serpents; and if they drink anything deadly, it will by no means hurt them; they will lay hands on the sick, and they will recover.

47

Together these portions of Scripture reveal important aspects of Jesus' authority and how it operates in kingdom work. In addition to reiterating His supreme authority in both the heavenly and earthly realms, Jesus delegates that authority to His disciples. Those whom He has commissioned have been given use of His name and the power it carries to cast out demons, speak in tongues, lay hands on the sick, and take dominion over the works of darkness. While these instructions were first given to the original disciples, they apply to believers today for the continued advancement of God's kingdom.

THE NAME OF JESUS IN THE BOOK OF ACTS

There are examples in Scripture of how the apostles demonstrated the authority in the name of Jesus during the early days of the church. Obedient to Jesus' instructions in the Great Commission, they took His authority and carried the kingdom into all the world using the power of His name. As a result, they saw people saved, healed, and delivered.

On the day of Pentecost when Peter preached to the crowds, he recalled the power of the name of Jesus and admonished people to be baptized in that name.

> Then Peter said to them, "Repent, and let every one of you be baptized *in the name of Jesus Christ* for the remission of sins; and you shall receive the gift of the Holy Spirit."
> —ACTS 2:38, EMPHASIS ADDED

Later, when Peter and John were addressing the Sanhedrin, they also admonished that salvation comes through the name of Jesus. They preached, "Nor is there salvation in any other, for *there is no other name* under heaven given among men by which we must be saved" (Acts 4:12, emphasis added).

In Acts 3, Peter uses the name of Jesus when praying for a lame man he met on the street:

> And a certain man lame from his mother's womb was carried, whom they laid daily at the gate of the temple which is called Beautiful, to ask alms from those who entered the temple; who, seeing Peter and John about to go into the temple, asked for alms. And fixing his eyes on him, with John, Peter said, "Look at us." So he gave them his attention, expecting to receive something from them. Then Peter said, "Silver and gold I do not have, but what I do have I give you: *In the name of Jesus Christ of Nazareth*, rise up and walk."
>
> And he took him by the right hand and lifted him up, and immediately his feet and ankle bones received strength. So he, leaping up, stood and walked and entered the temple with them—walking, leaping, and praising God.
>
> —ACTS 3:2–8, EMPHASIS ADDED

Peter recognized the power of the name of Jesus, used it, and obtained results in praying over the sick man. When news of the miracle spread throughout the city, Peter explained it in verse 16 by saying, "And His name, through faith in His name, has made this man strong, whom you see and know." It was the name's authority coupled with faith in the name that brought the healing.

Later in Acts, Paul encountered a demon-possessed young woman and cast out the spirit using the name of Jesus:

> Now it happened, as we went to prayer, that a certain slave girl possessed with a spirit of divination met us, who brought her masters much profit by fortune-telling. This girl followed Paul and us, and cried out, saying, "These men are the servants of the Most High God, who proclaim to us the way of salvation." And this she did for many days. But Paul, greatly annoyed, turned and said to the spirit, "I command you *in the name of Jesus Christ* to come out of her." And he came out that very hour.
> —ACTS 16:16–18, EMPHASIS ADDED

In obedience to the Great Commission, Paul used the authority in Jesus' name and set a girl free from demon possession!

As the disciples learned to use the authority Jesus delegated to them through the use of His name, tremendous things happened. The Word of God hasn't changed, and the power available to the early church is available to us today.

SUBMISSION TO AUTHORITY

In our discussion regarding the flow of authority, we've seen how authority flows from above in heaven to the earth below and from the spiritual realm to the natural realm. We've also seen how authority flows through the use of Jesus' name. There is yet another principle that governs the flow of authority, and that is submission to authority. In order for authority to work effectively in our lives, we have to learn how to both submit to Christ's authority and accept the authority He has delegated to us.

Perhaps one of the clearest pictures we see in the Bible regarding this relationship between authority and submission is found in Matthew 8. Jesus had just entered the city of Capernaum when a Roman centurion approached Him. Pleading with Him, the centurion said, "Lord, my servant is lying at home paralyzed, dreadfully tormented" (v. 6). In response, Jesus told the man, "I will come and heal him" (v. 7).

Astoundingly, the centurion answered, "Lord, I am not worthy that You should come under my roof. But only speak a word, and my servant will be healed. For I also am a man *under authority*, having soldiers under me. And I say to this one, 'Go,' and he goes; and to another, 'Come,' and he comes; and to my servant, 'Do this,' and he does it" (vv. 8–9, emphasis added).

Jesus marveled at the centurion's words and instructed him, "Go your way; and as you have believed, so let it be done for you." Then the verse says, "And his servant was healed that same hour" (v. 13).

Although this centurion was a Gentile, he believed in the Lord Jesus. He also understood the significance of authority and its relation to action, recognizing that authority is the ability and power to act. As part of the Roman army, the centurion had to work with superiors. He was accountable to respond to orders from his commanding officers, who were above him in authority and responsible for making weightier decisions. He also had to work with people who were under his authority. Although this group of men was of a lower rank and presumably less influential, they also had to respond correctly to any orders given to them.

As a military man, the centurion recognized the proper flow of authority. When he received orders from higher up, he had to obey. He understood that to be in authority one must recognize he or she is under authority; the authority flows from above. Likewise, when the centurion gave orders to the soldiers underneath him, they had to obey. In the military, obedience to a superior wasn't a choice but a required action, regardless of rank or status.

When it came to the healing of his servant, the centurion recognized that Jesus had authority over sickness. That's why it was so easy for him to believe the spoken word of Jesus in this situation. Because he was a man of natural authority who was also under authority, the centurion recognized the spiritual authority Jesus carried and was able to respond to it in faith. He took action by believing what Jesus said would be done. As a result, his servant was healed.

This story not only shows us how third-heaven authority works, but it also reveals how necessary authority is in the operation of faith. The highest authority begins with Jesus and is delegated to us from above. As we surrender to Jesus' authority without question, like a soldier submits to his commanding officer, we are empowered to carry out His authority on the earth.

THE LORD'S AUTHORITY

The Bible is full of additional scriptures that reveal the supreme authority given to Jesus. He has authority positionally from heaven. The Lord said, "Heaven is My throne, and earth is My footstool" (Acts 7:49). And we read later in Acts, "God, who made the world and everything in it, since He is Lord of heaven and earth, does not dwell in temples made with hands" (Acts 17:24). Even before the fall of man and the emergence of sin in the world, Jesus saw Satan fall like lightning from heaven (Luke 10:18).

Jesus Himself had to submit to the Father's authority during His earthly ministry, which included being crucified. As a result of His obedience, He was exalted to a place of authority after His resurrection:

> ...who, being in the form of God, did not consider it robbery to be equal with God, but made Himself of no reputation, taking the form of a bondservant, and coming in the likeness of men. And being found in appearance as a man, He humbled Himself and became obedient to the point of death, even the death of the cross. Therefore God also has highly exalted Him and given Him the name which is above every name, that at the name of Jesus every knee should bow, of those in heaven, and of those on earth, and of those under the earth, and that every tongue should confess that Jesus Christ is Lord, to the glory of God the Father.
>
> —PHILIPPIANS 2:6–11

Before He went to the cross, Jesus delegated His authority to the church. He told His disciples, "And I will give you the keys of the kingdom of heaven, and whatever you bind on earth will be bound in heaven, and whatever you loose on earth will be loosed in heaven" (Matt. 16:19). In the Greek text, the word translated "bind" means to declare unlawful or lock away, and the word translated "loose" means to declare lawful or to unlock.[1]

The verse also can be translated, "Whatever you bind (declare to be improper and unlawful) on earth must be what is already bound in heaven; and whatever you loose (declare lawful) on earth must be what is already loosed in heaven" (Matt. 16:19, AMPC). Because the authority flows from heaven above to earth below, the church has the delegated power from heaven to bind, loose, and command things in the realm of the spirit. As authority has been given to Jesus, so He has delegated that authority to us on the earth.

COMMISSIONED WITH AUTHORITY

Each of us has a specific kingdom assignment that we've been delegated the authority to carry out. We have not been given the authority to carry out someone else's assignment. This is why prayer and intimacy with Jesus are so critical. As we will see later, His will for us flows out of that intimacy.

Although I pray that you have many of them, you don't need an unusual, supernatural experience or vision to receive your assignment in the kingdom. God placed His Spirit within you at the new birth, and you already carry His new nature inside you. He has also given you His Word, which provides you with the instruction, correction, wisdom, and revelation you need to mature in your walk with God and execute your assignment. The Holy Spirit will give you further wisdom and instruction as you meditate on the Word and pray in the Spirit.

The Word itself is a commission from heaven. That's why it's so important to become a student of the Word, a workman who is not ashamed and who can properly divide truth from error (2 Tim. 2:15). By feeding on the Word daily, you're building a solid foundation of truth in your heart. You won't be swayed by various winds of doctrine because the Word of God is your anchor. God's Word will hold you steady in times of uncertainty, chaos, and confusion, and it will protect you from the deception and error that will arise in the last days.

If you're unsure of direction, the Word of God will reveal to you the right path for your life. It has the power to distinguish the voice of God from the clamoring of your soul (Heb. 4:12). It will reveal what is truly God's plan for you while exposing the thoughts and intentions coming from the soulish realm—or those things that are the results of your own reasoning and emotions.

When the Lord highlights a promise to you in His Word, you can receive it in your heart by faith. You can act on it simply because you understand the authority inherent in God's Word. By receiving God's Word as the authority in your life, you can then put actions to what you've read or heard, which will cause you to see God's promises come to pass!

When the angel appeared to Mary and told her she would have the Christ Child, Mary didn't understand with her natural mind how such a miraculous birth could happen. She hadn't been intimate with a man. There was no physical means whereby this promise could occur.

However, the angel told her, "The Holy Spirit will come upon you, and the power of the Highest will overshadow you; therefore, also, that Holy One who is to be born will be called the Son of God" (Luke 1:35). In other words, the angel was telling Mary, "Something supernatural is going to happen to you. This is going to be done from heaven by the authority of God."

As Mary recognized the magnitude of the miracle, her faith took hold of the words she heard from the angel, and she replied, "Let it be to me according to your word" (Luke 1:38). Mary's faith hooked up with God's word spoken to her. She acknowledged the authority of the word and received God's supernatural power. As a result, the miracle occurred.

The Holy Spirit will most often speak through that still, small voice in your inner being. Sometimes He may speak in a louder voice. The Lord may give us visions, dreams, or an angelic visitation. All of these supernatural means of heaven work together to impart God's plans to us.

Third-heaven authority belongs to you just as much as it does to me. I believe the church has only tapped into a tiny sliver of the power and authority that is available in Jesus. It's time for us to rise up and advance the kingdom of heaven with great power and authority on the earth!

CHAPTER 5

LEVELS OF SPIRITUAL INFLUENCE

A s WE DIG deeper into authority, we'll find there are
four different types of authority. God designed these
levels of authority to work together. They keep His creation, both in the natural and spiritual realms, in proper
order and balance.

NATURAL AUTHORITY

The first type of authority is what I call the authority of
mankind. This refers to the overall responsibility we have
as humans over our environment, God's creation, and the
works of our own hands.

> Then God said, "Let Us make man in Our image,
> according to Our likeness; let them have dominion
> over the fish of the sea, over the birds of the air, and
> over the cattle, over all the earth and over every
> creeping thing that creeps on the earth." So God
> created man in His own image; in the image of God
> He created him; male and female He created them.
> Then God blessed them, and God said to them, "Be
> fruitful and multiply; fill the earth and subdue it;
> have dominion over the fish of the sea, over the
> birds of the air, and over every living thing that
> moves on the earth."
>
> —GENESIS 1:26–28

This authority continues to this day. Psalm 8:3–8 also describes the natural authority God has given us:

> When I consider Your heavens, the work of Your fingers, the moon and the stars, which You have ordained, what is man that You are mindful of him, and the son of man that You visit him? For You have made him a little lower than the angels, and You have crowned him with glory and honor. You have made him to have dominion over the works of Your hands; You have put all things under his feet, all sheep and oxen—even the beasts of the field, the birds of the air, and the fish of the sea that pass through the paths of the seas.

From the beginning God gave Adam and Eve dominion over all the works of His hands. This authority extended even to space exploration, which wasn't accessed until modern times. However, God saw the end from the beginning and knew that man would land on the moon one day! Everything within the realm of the natural creation God gave mankind authority to rule, reign, explore, discover, cultivate, develop, and ultimately to *bless*. Have dominion!

SPIRITUAL AUTHORITY

The second type of authority is what we call the authority of the believer. This is authority we exercise in the spiritual realm, the domain of spiritual beings such as angels and demons, as we discussed in chapter 1.

Jesus mentioned this authority in Luke 10 when He told the disciples: "Behold, I give you the authority to trample on serpents and scorpions, and over all the power of the enemy, and nothing shall by any means hurt you" (v. 19). This authority empowers us to gain victory over the enemy in spiritual warfare. It is the authority through which we bind, loose, and release God's creative power into the earth. This kind of authority brings heaven's will onto the planet. Jesus won this authority through His death on the cross, and He delegated it back to us, His disciples.

The problem arose when sin came into the earth through Adam's disobedience in the Garden of Eden. Consequently, man's spiritual authority was handed over to Satan. He then became the god of this world and now holds earthly kingdoms in his hand. We see this clearly in Luke 4:5–7 when Satan tempted Jesus in the wilderness:

> Then the devil, taking Him up on a high mountain, showed Him all the kingdoms of the world in a moment of time. And the devil said to Him, "All this authority I will give You, and their glory; for this has been delivered to me, and I give it to whomever I wish. Therefore, if You will worship before me, all will be Yours."

If you continue reading the passage, you'll see that Jesus didn't dispute those words. What Satan offered was an actual temptation. Jesus knew He'd have to shed His blood to legally purchase the authority Satan flaunted in His face. There was no easy way out. Jesus would have to go to the cross.

When Adam sinned against God in the Garden of Eden, he opened the door to the curse. Adam's fall gave Satan authority in the natural world, and he introduced spiritual death, sin, sickness, poverty, wars, and every kind of wickedness. The enemy came to steal, kill, and destroy humanity in every possible way. It was all unleashed into the earth the day Adam sinned.

Thankfully, God had a solution! He had a plan of redemption that would transfer all spiritual power and authority back to Jesus through what we call the finished work of the cross. Jesus willingly submitted Himself to the horrible pains of death. He took the punishment for every sin ever committed. He actually became a curse for us when He laid down His life and died (Gal. 3:13). Then on the third day, when the Holy Spirit rushed into hell and raised Jesus from the dead, Jesus disarmed Satan and destroyed his works. Our Lord paraded Satan and his cohorts in the spiritual realm as vanquished foes. God gave His Son the name that is above every name, and all spiritual authority was bestowed upon Jesus.

Then Jesus did an amazing thing: He turned around and handed that authority back to us! He paid the price with His own blood to reclaim the authority mankind lost through sin, and then gave that authority to every person who would receive Jesus Christ as Lord and Savior. To this day, when we use our God-given authority, we enforce this powerful victory. This was God's plan of salvation! (See Mark 16:17, John 3:8, and Colossians 2:15.)

In this current time continuum, Satan is the god of this world. He still governs the fallen belief system that pervades the earth today. There is still sin in the world, and there is still wickedness, darkness, and spiritual death. This is why people need to accept Jesus as Lord and come into the kingdom of God; it's so the power of darkness can be broken off their lives.

Once you become born again, you regain your spiritual

authority. Jesus took that authority from Satan with the intention of giving it back to you. He doesn't need that authority in heaven. He endured the cross so you could be saved and walk in spiritual authority over the devil here on earth.

The moment you put your trust in Him, you become a new creation in Christ Jesus. At that point, you have authority in Christ to exercise dominion over the devil and all the works of darkness. Jesus said "these signs will follow those who believe" and then described the power of the gospel. He ensured that you could be more than a conqueror. And this is why the Great Commission applies to you. With the authority given to you when you were born again, you have the power to cast out demons, speak with new tongues, take up serpents (evil spirits), and lay hands on the sick. The miraculous works of Jesus in His earthly ministry are the same works you can do today as a born-again believer!

POSITIONAL AUTHORITY

The third type of authority is the authority of position, or what one might call the authority of responsibility. This relates to the specific way God intended blessings to flow from heaven through relationships on earth. In other words, this is God's created order for how power is to be executed in the relational realm.

We saw this earlier in chapter 4 in the example of the centurion. He was a man both *in* authority and *under* authority. His understanding of the lines of authority allowed him to have faith in Jesus' command. He believed the only thing Jesus had to do was speak the word and his servant would be healed. The centurion under-stood authority, and Jesus marveled at his *faith*, saying, "Assuredly, I say to you, I have not found such great faith, not even in Israel!" (Matt. 8:10).

Positional authority is God's divine authority delegated through leadership. We see it in government, family, the local church, and the marketplace. The Bible instructs us to pray for those in leadership, "for kings and all who are in authority, that we may lead a quiet and peaceable life in all godliness and reverence" (1 Tim. 2:2). We are also commanded to honor our leaders because of their posi-tion. That includes those who cover us spiritually such as pastors and other spiritual leaders.

> Remember those who rule over you, who have spoken the word of God to you, whose faith follow, considering the outcome of their conduct....Obey those who rule over you, and be submissive, for they watch out for your souls, as those who must give account.
> —HEBREWS 13:7, 17

In Ephesians 5, Paul discusses positional authority at work in a number of interpersonal relationships, including the relationships between husband and wife, parent and child, and boss and employee. While these relationships may seem limited to the natural realm, there are strong spiritual dynamics involved in them. Heaven's blessings are released when our hearts for one another align with God's heart. This releases a divine flow and positions us to receive peace, joy, safety, protection, and answers to prayer.

If we are appointed to a position of leadership in the home or church, in government, or on the job, we must recognize the responsibility that goes with it. Submit yourself to God so He can empower you to love, honor, and respect those who are entrusted to your care. A great picture of this is Paul's admonishment to husbands to "love your wives, just as Christ also loved the church and gave Himself for her" (Eph. 5:25). In this case, authority or leadership means becoming a servant.

Rejecting God-given lines of authority is called lawlessness, and lawlessness releases demonic influences into relationships, causing damage and destruction. This applies to those *in* authority as well as those *under* authority. But be encouraged! The correction for abuse is not *disuse* but *right* use.

THE AUTHORITY OF THE GLORY

The fourth type of authority is that which is contained within God's glory. It's the supernatural release of God's glory and may be expressed as God's manifest presence, supernatural visitations, visions, and other spiritual experiences. When we experience these kinds of encounters, God sovereignly moves by His power to bring change.

Every time God manifests Himself, He changes what He is touching. In other words, whenever God shows up or wherever His glory is found, something is going to happen. A miracle of some magnitude will occur. People may experience salvation, receive the baptism of the Holy Spirit, be healed, or be delivered from demons. God's presence may also so saturate a particular atmosphere that people can hardly stand up—a physical manifestation similar to what the priests in the Old Testament experienced when God's glory filled the temple. (See 1 Kings 8:10–13, AMP.) Today we can experience God's manifested glory collectively during a church service or individually during a time of prayer or worship.

There have been times when God's glory manifested in our church services. In those times, His presence became tangible and thick and touched everyone in the room. You couldn't escape or deny it. Even unbelievers crash under God's presence when it comes like that. People weep, laugh, or even fall on the floor. We sometimes use the phrases "being drunk in the Spirit" or "falling out under the power" to describe the physical reactions people have as they encounter God's powerful presence and manifest glory. It is also in the atmosphere of God's glory that many experience visions, dreams, impartations, or angelic visitations. All these supernatural experiences result from God invading our lives and the natural realm around us.

God never moves without a reason, and when His glory manifests in such a way, an impartation is given. This may be in the form of a revelation of God's Word, a fresh anointing and imbuing of power, or a new God-breathed assignment. We come out of such experiences with authority to carry out whatever He has instructed us to do.

When I was caught up to the third heaven, I wasn't sitting around asking God for a visitation. I was deeply engaged in the act of intercession at the prayer meeting. Recently, I had a supernatural encounter in which an angel touched my lips with a warm substance. Simultaneously the Lord spoke to me and renewed my assignment to teach His children third-heaven authority. When the angel touched my lips, it felt like warm honey flowed into my belly. That was a manifestation of God's glory that left me with the authority to carry out my assignment to teach what He revealed to me.

When we gather together in the Lord, even if there are just two or three, we create an atmosphere for encounters with God's glory. This is why it's important for us to regularly meet as a group of believers and seek God's face in prayer and worship. As we wait on the Lord, we give Him an opportunity to manifest Himself among us both individually and corporately.

Unfortunately, some of God's people are afraid of the glory. They think it's emotionalism and too undignified. But denying the glory is rejecting the presence and touch of God, which is an expression of His authority.

The first recorded demonstration of God's manifest presence touching the early church is found in Acts 2. This is when the Holy Spirit was first poured out upon the disciples on the day of Pentecost. After they experienced this powerful touch from the Holy Spirit, they were so overcome with God's presence that onlookers thought they were drunk! But they weren't drunk; they were overcome by God's glory. They were also transformed and empowered to preach the gospel with boldness. As a result, thousands were born again that day!

Another example of an encounter with God's glory is found in Acts 10, where Peter had a vision of a sheet being lowered with unclean animals. To the natural mind this was a strange occurrence, but it was a supernatural vision that gave Peter revelation. Later we find that because of this encounter, the Gentiles were brought into the church through Cornelius' household.

Paul the apostle also experienced supernatural

manifestations of God's glory. Acts 16 records one such example when Paul had a vision in the middle of the night of a man from Macedonia saying, "Come over here and help us." As a result of this vision, Paul traveled to Macedonia and preached Christ to those in that region. By cooperating with God's authority as expressed in the glory, Paul received his next ministry assignment and the power to fulfill what God had called him to do.

The Old Testament also contains several examples of people experiencing the manifest glory of God. Ezekiel recorded this encounter:

> Like the appearance of a rainbow in a cloud on a rainy day, so was the appearance of the brightness all around it. This was the appearance of the likeness of the glory of the LORD. So when I saw it, I fell on my face, and I heard a voice of One speaking.
> —EZEKIEL 1:28

Daniel described his experience in the presence of God this way:

> Now, as he was speaking with me, I was in a deep sleep with my face to the ground; but he touched me, and stood me upright. And he said, "Look, I am making known to you what shall happen in the latter time of the indignation; for at the appointed time the end shall be."
> —DANIEL 8:18–19

When the prophets of the Old Testament encountered God's presence, Scripture often notes that they fell back or on their faces before the Lord. In those overpowering moments they received instruction from God and were empowered to fulfill their assignments. These men were mightily touched by the Lord and completely changed in that one moment in God's glory.

As we can see from Scripture, anytime someone encountered the glory or presence of God, something powerful happened. God is the same today. He never changes. His glory still touches people, changing and empowering them. We can be sure that whenever we encounter the glory of God, He imparts something fresh and new into our spirits. We come out of each of those precious experiences with a new authority to release into the earth!

THIRD-HEAVEN AUTHORITY

In essence, third-heaven authority is not so much about a new level of authority but having the revelation to walk in and release all four types of authority we've just discussed. It's about seeing authority from God's perspective above and walking correctly in what He has delegated to us in both the natural and spiritual realms.

Our new perspective causes us to use our authority and power more, thereby increasing the results. This is why Colossians 3:1–2 reminds us, "If then you were raised with Christ, seek those things which are above, where Christ is, sitting at the right hand of God. Set your mind on things above, not on things on the earth." Remember, if you are in Christ, you are sitting right there with Him. (See Ephesians 1:19–20 and Ephesians 2:6.)

No More Sin-Consciousness

One of the key components of having the right perspective from this heavenly place is being free from the dominion or consciousness of sin. Our new life in Christ changes us from the inside out and empowers us to walk freely in the righteousness provided for us in Christ.

The writer of Hebrews explains:

> For the law, having a shadow of the good things to come, and not the very image of the things, can never with these same sacrifices, which they offer continually year by year, make those who approach perfect. For then would they not have ceased to be offered? For the worshipers, once purified, would have had no more consciousness of sins. But in those sacrifices there is a reminder of sins every year.... Let us draw near with a true heart in full assurance of faith, having our hearts sprinkled from an evil conscience and our bodies washed with pure water.
> —Hebrews 10:1–3, 22

Seeing ourselves as evil sinners is tied to the earth. It's an earthly, fleshly perspective that robs believers of their authority by causing them to focus on the outer man. Sin-consciousness is constantly seeing ourselves as wicked, unworthy, and controlled by our flesh. It is a disqualifying mindset that seeks to make us "worthy" through religious works. Jesus qualified us by His good works and "sprinkled" us from a sin-consciousness with His own blood.

Seeing ourselves as righteous through Christ, on the other hand, is tied to heaven's perspective, where our true, eternal identity dwells. This awareness allows us to see everything from that higher position of being in Him. It is a perspective that the Holy Spirit builds inside us through revelation and experience. As we soak in the Word and experience the Holy Spirit's presence in our lives, our perspective shifts away from an earthly vantage point. Our minds begin a lifelong process of being renewed to the holiness of God—His wisdom, righteousness, truth, ways, and will.

This constant transformation of our thinking raises our perspective higher and higher so that we understand more clearly all that Christ has done for us in His finished work at Calvary. We've heard it said, "Don't be so heavenly minded that you are of no earthly good." That is not scriptural. We are to set our minds on things above (Col. 3:2). The truth is, until we are heavenly minded and understand our perfected identity from that perspective, we won't be of much earthly good for the kingdom of God.

Dipping back into Ephesians for a moment, the first half of the book is basically Paul telling us who we are, our identity in Christ. The second half of Ephesians is Paul telling us to walk like who we are! By continuing to gain an increased understanding of who we are as new creations in Christ, we allow the Holy Spirit to purge our hearts and consciousness from the things of the flesh, such as condemnation, guilt, and fear. As we become loosed of the things that debase us, our consciousness is being cleansed and recalibrated to think in line with the new creation. This causes our spirit man on the inside to soar with the Holy Spirit rather than to be dominated by the flesh and sin-consciousness.

To put it simply, this is what third-heaven authority is all about. It covers every part of our existence and our walk with the Lord. Yes, it is knowing how to walk in victory in spiritual warfare, and it encompasses our authority over the enemy. But third-heaven authority also relates to our ability to release the creative aspects of the kingdom of heaven into the earth. It is what perceives the will of God and surrenders to it. It recognizes God's divine order of authority and cooperates with it in both the natural and spiritual realms. It is the ability to tap into the flow of God's power and release it into all areas of our lives.

My heart's prayer for you is that your spirit would awaken to the awesomeness of God's immense power available to you. As Paul prayed for the Ephesian believers, I pray also for you: May the eyes of your understanding be enlightened so that you may know the exceeding greatness of His power that is at work in and for you. May third-heaven revelation be granted to you by the power of the Holy Spirit!

CHAPTER 6

WALKING IN HEAVENLY AUTHORITY

EVERYTHING WE'VE TALKED about thus far is foundational. But how do we apply third-heaven authority practically, flip the switch, and see results? In this chapter, I'd like to answer that question.

BELIEVE IN SPIRITUAL AUTHORITY

Before you can do anything, you must believe you have authority. I know that sounds super simple, but unbelief is the killer of God things. The writer of Hebrews wrote that "without faith it is impossible to please God, for he who comes to God must believe that He exists and that He is a rewarder of those who diligently seek Him" (Heb. 11:6, MEV).

Walking in third-heaven authority begins with diligently pursuing the things of God by faith. The reward can be several things, starting with God Himself, who rewards us with His truth and presence. The reward can also be walking in His third-heaven authority. Without faith there is no way you will ever walk in the authority God designed for you. Luke wrote, "When the Son of Man comes, will He find faith on the earth?" (Luke 18:8, MEV). Faith is what moves God, and it is what God is looking for.

When unbelief creeps in, it causes you to operate only from your natural mind and sight. But things are not always as they seem. You must believe you have spiritual authority given to you by Jesus, that through it you can bind and loose in the name of Jesus, and that when you exercise your authority God is working and changing things even if you don't immediately see results.

Jesus told His disciples, "Assuredly, I say to you, whatever you bind on earth will be bound in heaven, and whatever you loose on earth will be loosed in heaven" (Matt. 18:18). Do you believe Jesus' words? I want to challenge you right now to believe Him! When we loose things on earth, we are exercising the creative aspect of third-heaven authority to release the kingdom of God into the natural realm. In the beginning, God spoke and unleashed a spiritual creative force that caused physical matter to emerge from nothing. Because we are made in the image and likeness of God, His creative power abides in us, and we can speak with creative power. I learned a long time ago that things pertaining to the kingdom of God and the spiritual realm must be released into the physical atmosphere, into people's lives, and into situations and circumstances, creating change.

Scripture is what activates or sparks the ignition of faith: "So then faith comes by hearing, and hearing by the word of God" (Rom. 10:17, MEV). We speak the Word, and faith rises. But in order to speak the Word, we have to know the Word. Second Timothy 2:15 instructs us to "be diligent to present yourself approved to God, a worker who does not need to be ashamed, rightly dividing the word of truth." There's that word *diligent* again. The things of God come to those who are diligent. As we diligently study God's Word, the Holy Spirit will illuminate our hearts and bring revelation of truth to our spirits. That truth also stores up in our minds, so the Holy Spirit can bring the Word to our remembrance when we need it. Understanding all of this is critical to walking in the authority that is ours.

Having a true revelation from Scripture of who you are in Christ, what He has given you, and what He's capable of doing in you keeps you from believing the enemy's lies. Satan can lead you astray in your thinking, which will eventually take you down the wrong path and cause you to engage in ungodly actions. This is why it's so important to always have a solid scriptural foundation undergirding your mind and heart.

The revelation of the Word imparted to you by the Holy Spirit defines the areas in which you can use your authority as well as your capacity to release that authority. In other words, to the degree that you believe it, you can walk in it. Reading God's Word, meditating on it, and receiving revelation from it in faith are the prerequisites to walking in third-heaven authority.

BE FILLED WITH THE HOLY SPIRIT

Another prerequisite for releasing our authority is being filled with the Holy Spirit with the evidence of speaking in tongues. I can't stress this enough. In recent years there's been a move away from the need to pray in the Spirit with what many call our heavenly language. This is huge, because praying in supernatural tongues is our secret weapon and the doorway to the realm of the Spirit. Paul told the Corinthian church, "For he who speaks in a tongue does not speak to men but to God, for no one understands him; however, in the spirit he speaks mysteries" (1 Cor. 14:2). The word *mysteries* in this verse is the Greek term *mystērion*, which refers to revealed secrets.

There are hidden secrets in the kingdom of God that are revealed to those who have the Holy Spirit and are walking in Him, reading God's Word, and experiencing the revelation that is coming forth. When we pray in other tongues, we are praying out the mysteries of God's plan.

Because praying in tongues is such a vital component to our walk with God, it behooves us to pray in our prayer language every day. I recommend praying in tongues at least fifteen minutes every day. Then as praying in the Spirit becomes a daily habit, you'll soon increase your prayer time without even realizing it, sometimes praying for an hour or more. Praying often in other tongues causes you to draw from the well of the Holy Spirit deep inside you and be strengthened, refreshed, and renewed in your own spirit. It becomes "addictive," and you'll experience supernatural power and quiet peace as you pray.

While you're praying in tongues, the Holy Spirit will implant wise thoughts, breakthrough ideas, and unique direction. Some days you pray in tongues by faith because you're tired and don't feel anything. In those times, your mind is unfruitful while your spirit prays. Then hours or sometimes days later there's a sudden Holy Spirit manifestation or breakthrough. That is a direct result of consistently praying in the Spirit, even when you feel nothing.

According to Jude 20, you can build yourself up on your most holy faith simply by praying in the Holy Spirit. In addition to praying out the mysteries and divine secrets of God's plan, praying in tongues enhances your spiritual perception. You become more sensitive to the leading of the Spirit of God, and you're able to discern His plan more easily. Everyone I know who truly operates in the power of the Spirit of God practices speaking in tongues.

RELEASE YOUR AUTHORITY

Once you have activated third-heaven authority, you must release it. There are three keys to accomplishing this.

1. Be obedient to the Word and pray in the name of Jesus. The first and primary way we release our authority is simply by praying in obedience to the Word and in the name of Jesus. Again, it's so simple, but sometimes the simplest things are the most neglected. The Bible tells us that if we lay hands on the sick, they shall recover (Mark 16:18). We just need to do that, expecting God's healing power to be released whenever we pray for those who are sick. The Bible also commands us to "go into all the world and preach the gospel to every creature" (Mark 16:15). By being obedient to Scripture and preaching the gospel, we will see people receive salvation through Jesus.

Similarly, when you "resist the devil" as the Word says, "he will flee from you" (Jas. 4:7, MEV). That's a promise. Obedience releases God's authority over the enemy. He has no choice but to flee from us! Are you actively resisting, or are you passively being conformed to the devil's schemes against you? The same is true of the instruction the Bible gives to pray in the name of Jesus (John 14:13–14; John 16:23–24). When we do so in obedience and faith, we release God's power and authority into the situation.

We touched on the importance of the name of Jesus in chapter 4, but I'd like to share here a few more things regarding praying in His name. In the early days of my ministry, I was traveling to another city to hold a meeting. I'd only been in ministry a short while, and I was still learning some things about prayer, authority, and God's power. During that time, the Holy Spirit revealed to me something about the name of Jesus I have never forgotten.

At that point, like most Christians, I had already learned how to put my faith in the name of Jesus. I knew demons had to obey and flee when they were rebuked in Jesus' name. I understood that sickness and disease had to leave bodies in the name of Jesus Christ. As a younger man, filled with faith and authority, I was on fire and ready to see God's power move when I ministered.

Well, during one particular meeting, I preached on the power in the name of Jesus. After my message was over, I invited people who needed a miracle to come forward for prayer. A large group of people responded and gathered at the front in a prayer line, and I began to pray for them one by one.

When I started to pray for the first person in line, my faith was so anchored in the power of the name of Jesus. I reached out, touched the person on the forehead, and said, "Be healed in the name of Jesus." Boom! The power of God hit, and the person fell to the floor under that power, later testifying that he was healed.

When I came to the next person in line, I could tell the anointing was increasing. As I reached this man, touched him on the forehead, and began to pray, all I could get out was the word "Be" before he also hit the floor under the power of the Holy Spirit.

I came to the third person and simply reached my hand toward her forehead, and she too went down in the power of the Spirit. I went over to the next one, and before I could even raise my hand, I just looked at him, and he also went down in the power. Like a row of dominoes, one after another after another people continued to fall out under the power of the Holy Spirit even before I could lay hands on them or say, "Be healed in the name of Jesus." All were receiving their healing supernaturally as the power of God was visibly manifesting.

As I watched in amazement, I pondered the events of that prayer line and asked the Lord how these people were receiving healing even before I was able to say "in Jesus' name." The Lord whispered, "Aren't you in My name? Didn't you come to this city in My name? Didn't you preach that sermon in My name? Aren't you praying for these people in My name?"

I responded, "Yes, Lord."

He replied, "Then that fulfills the requirement. You are doing it in My name whether you get to mouth the word or not. Just believe in My name, and My power will be on you. It will bring about the authority for performing the miraculous. Yes, use My name, but don't be worried if you don't get to say it." This was a powerful lesson I learned that day.

The easiest way to walk in God's authority is by being obedient. Because you are already seated with Him in heavenly places, when you obey Him and act on what His Word says to do, results follow. They must, because God honors His Word. People will get saved, strongholds will be broken, the sick will be healed, and miracles will happen. Demons will be cast out because of your obedience to the Lord. You will have success in exercising authority simply due to your obedience to the Word and your faith in the name of Jesus.

2. See yourself praying from heaven's perspective. The next key to walking in third-heaven authority is to pray while consciously in your heart seeing yourself above looking down on each situation. We've talked about this throughout the previous pages, but it comes down to this: When you pray, see yourself as seated with Christ in heavenly places looking down to the earth below. From this perspective you will see yourself above the circumstances, not beneath them. Of course, this does not come naturally and takes practice.

Not too long ago, a woman approached me after a service and shared her testimony with me. She said, "Pastor Mike, I've heard you preach on third-heaven authority. I may not have experienced a heavenly vision like you, but I now understand how to pray more effectively after hearing your teaching. In fact, something happened on the night I listened to you explain third-heaven authority. Something changed inside me, and the Holy Spirit is working in my heart. Since then, every time I pray in my personal prayer closet, pray for someone to be healed, rebuke a demon, or bind or loose something, I feel a lifting on the inside of me. In my heart, there's a new perspective. I see myself rising up and looking down on the situation from above, not below like I used to all these years."

This dear lady received the revelation of third-heaven authority. She saw herself seated with Christ in heavenly places. She understood that her position is above the circumstances and not below them. And because a new perspective has entered her heart, her prayers are more effective than before.

Sometimes we need to allow the Holy Spirit to paint His image on our hearts, much like an artist would paint a picture on a canvas. The Lord uses this imagery to help us understand biblical truths. Throughout His earthly ministry, even Jesus used parables to reveal certain truths and teach His disciples lessons of the kingdom. I believe imagery is a language of the Spirit and something God can use to help us understand complex truths pertaining to His kingdom.

3. Yield to the Holy Spirit. The third key to releasing heaven's authority in your life is to yield to the Holy Spirit and let Him have control. This is a matter of being sensitive to His voice, finding where He's flowing, and going with it. When we do, we tap into His authority. There are times when the Holy Spirit will begin to prompt you through the manifestation of the gifts of the Spirit such as prophecy, words of wisdom, or a word of knowledge. Other times, He may give you a vision or dream. He may even move on you in an atmosphere where the glory of God is manifest. In any case, where the Spirit of God is moving, release your authority from there. Pray and decree while the anointing is flowing and the encounter is underway. By cooperating with Him, you can experience His authority in a higher dimension.

Years ago, I went to the Lord in prayer for a boy who was about eight years old. His family attended our church, and his parents didn't know what to do with him because he was uncontrollable. They had to lock him in his room at night; otherwise, he would sneak out of the house and run around the neighborhood, getting into trouble. At school he was a terror. He picked on other children and even attacked his teacher with a baseball bat.

As I prayed in tongues for the boy, I saw a vision. In the spirit, a rattlesnake appeared before me. It was as if the snake was afflicting the child and didn't want to let him go. The snake coiled and began to hiss, ready to strike. Suddenly, a sword appeared in my right hand, and I heard the Spirit of the Lord say, "Cut the head off the snake." I swung the sword in obedience, severing the snake's head from its body. Simultaneously, I said, "In Jesus' name, I command you to release the boy and set him free. I decree that he is delivered now." Then the vision ended.

Later that day I called the boy's parents and asked them to come to church early the following Sunday so we could pray for their son before the service. As I laid hands on the child, he was completely released from the torment. I understood that the deliverance had occurred when I prayed during the spiritual encounter and took authority over the demonic spirit. However, it manifested in the child's life when I laid hands on him at church.

The boy's parents were amazed that there was an immediate change in their son. He became the most loving child they could imagine. His teachers told them he was a totally different boy, and he started making friends with the other children at school. It's so important to flow with what the Holy Spirit is doing, even if it seems unorthodox.

If you're afraid of looking foolish or being mocked by others when yielding to the Holy Spirit, I encourage you to release those fears to the Lord. Yes, yielding to the Holy Spirit will sometimes be uncomfortable to you, much like wearing a new pair of shoes. However, the more you step out in faith to move with the Holy Spirit, the more His ways will become familiar to you. You can let go of what makes sense to your natural thinking and learn to flow into the deeper realms of the Spirit of God.

Because our natural minds rise up with excuses and search for what's reasonable, this is more difficult than it seems. The ways of the Spirit are often contrary to our natural thinking. Flowing with the Holy Spirit isn't something you do with your head, your natural mind, your reasoning, or your emotions. It is a response from your spirit to the Holy Spirit. It's important to recognize that God is a Spirit, and He speaks to your spirit by His Holy Spirit. Therefore, when you hear Him speak to you, it will be inside your spirit—in that deep place of your heart.

Over time, you will know that voice like you know your significant other's voice. When you hear your spouse over the phone or talking in a crowd, you instantly know who is speaking. Your response to the Holy Spirit from your own spirit may generate different outward expressions through your emotions, words, and physical body. But hearing, receiving, and responding to the Holy Spirit will always take place inside you—in your re-created spirit that has been born again and has received new life in Christ.

After learning to follow these three principles in obedience and faith, you'll be able to confidently step out into the moving of the Holy Spirit. Because you've developed a familiarity with Him by knowing the Word and praying daily in tongues, you'll be sensitive to His promptings when He desires to manifest one of the gifts of the Spirit through you. You'll also be more alert to His presence and more aware of what He wants you to do personally and when ministering to others.

CHAPTER 7

FIVE WAYS SATAN QUESTIONS YOUR AUTHORITY

As I write this book, it's been twelve years since the Lord caught me up into heaven and gave me the assignment to teach God's people third-heaven authority and all the related spiritual dynamics. I'm humbled and grateful. In those years, my spiritual life and sphere of ministry have grown exponentially, and thousands of believers have been empowered to walk in a greater sense of authority.

Jesus wants His body of believers to glimpse what things look like from the throne room. Unfortunately, instead of viewing things from heaven's viewpoint, many Christians are still focused on the natural things of this earth. That's where we live. It's also where Satan, the "god" of this world, has his domain. He is "the prince of the power of the air" (Eph. 2:2) and a principality we have to deal with down here. I've learned that his number one weapon is deceit.

Satan deceived Eve in the Garden of Eden by asking a question: "Now the serpent was more cunning than any beast of the field which the LORD God had made. And he said to the woman, 'Has God indeed said, "You shall not eat of every tree of the garden"?'" (Gen. 3:1). He knew the answer was yes, but he wasn't asking for himself. It was a strategy to cause Eve to doubt what God had said. Likewise with Jesus in the wilderness, Matthew 4:3 tells us, "Now when the tempter came to Him, he said, 'If You are the Son of God, command that these stones become bread.'" Of course Jesus is the Son of God! The tempter was attempting to sway the Lord. Unlike Eve, Jesus was grounded in the truth and refused to fall for Satan's trap.

The only reason Satan questions our authority is because he already knows we have authority over him. He wants to get believers to doubt God's Word and thus question their authority and disqualify themselves in their own minds. Don't fall for it!

A good place to begin looking at how Satan questions us is in a story about some religious leaders who questioned Jesus.

> Then they came again to Jerusalem. And as He was walking in the temple, the chief priests, the scribes, and the elders came to Him. And they said to Him, "By what *authority* are You doing these things? And who gave You this *authority* to do these things?"
>
> But Jesus answered and said to them, "I also will ask you one question; then answer Me, and I will tell you by what *authority* I do these things: The baptism of John—was it from heaven or from men? Answer Me."
>
> And they reasoned among themselves, saying, "If we say, 'From heaven,' He will say, 'Why then did you not believe him?' But if we say, 'From men'"— they feared the people, for all counted John to have been a prophet indeed. So they answered and said to Jesus, "We do not know."
>
> And Jesus answered and said to them, "Neither will I tell you by what *authority* I do these things."
>
> —MARK 11:27–33, EMPHASIS ADDED

The issue was authority. The religious leaders came to question Jesus and His authority. Why was He doing what He was doing, and who gave Him permission to do it? They believed they had all the authority and were the only ones who could give others permission to be involved in ministry. They weren't questioning Jesus' subjection to their office or the Jewish religious system. Jesus wasn't in rebellion to God's prescribed system of authority. He didn't launch any kind of insurrection and take over the temple or the synagogue. He didn't petition for the removal of any priests. Jesus was not violating any provision of the Levitical system. What He did was shine a light upon the religious leaders and their secret motives.

The spiritual dynamics of the kingdom that Jesus displayed were inconsistent with the religious leaders' attitude and the way they treated the people. Jesus was a threat to them. He taught the kingdom of God, love, liberty, and grace. He healed the sick, delivered the demonized, and fed the multitudes. Jesus gave hope and value to all the people, including the lowly and rejected. Yet He pointed out the sin and hypocrisy of those steeped in religious pride. Practically overnight, Jesus became the most popular man who had ever walked the planet. The people loved Him. All this caused the religious elite to burn with jealousy and question Jesus' authority.

Satan does the same thing today. He hates God's people, is jealous of us, and tries to paralyze us by questioning our authority. He whispers to us, "Who do you think you are? God's not listening to you. Who gave you authority? By what right are you doing these things? Where did you get the permission?" We are children of God, and our permission comes from Him. We have the power of God, the name of Jesus, and the Word of God at our disposal. We have the blood of Jesus backing us up. It's God's power and authority that we can rightfully claim for ourselves. Power is the *ability* to act. The power of God backs up everything we do. It's how God moves. Authority, on the other hand, is the *right* to act, or divine permission, and this has been delegated to us. However, our adversary Satan wants to keep us from believing and walking in what is rightfully ours.

There are five main tactics Satan uses to question your authority and get you to back down and just let the world run over you. Don't fall for any of them! As I share these tactics, I challenge you to listen to the Holy Spirit. Let Him reveal to your heart where any of these tactics has been at work, trying to shut you down. Jesus wants to set you free so your heart can soar like an eagle in the heavens. The Spirit of the Lord will reveal who God created you to be and what He has called you to do as you walk in His grace. Only by faith and His grace will you have the boldness to walk in third-heaven authority.

1. THE SPIRIT OF RELIGION

A religious spirit is the first tactic Satan uses to question your spiritual authority. Years ago, I did an in-depth Bible study from Genesis to Revelation, focusing on what I call the spirit of religion. It was interesting to discover that the serpent was associated with religious works. In Genesis, a loving God created mankind and called His creation "very good" (Gen. 1:31). Adam and Eve thrived in the Lord's grace until they disobeyed God by eating from the tree of the knowledge of good and evil. Through this violation,

Satan had an open door to introduce a performance-based system into the earth. Mankind was reduced to thinking they earned their significance through their performance. The lie then was that God could only accept those who earned His attention by what they did rather than who they were as His children.

God's grace is His unmerited favor and empowering presence, which enable us to be who He created us to be and do what He has called us to do. Grace is the relational structure of heaven. It is a heavenly system. Legalism and performance are the relational structure of hell. God operates by grace. Satan operates by performance, and performance clothed in religious garb is spiritually powerless. Like the tree Jesus cursed in Mark 11:13–14, it looks good but has no fruit.

Satan whispers in your ear, "Earn it. You have to take matters into your own hands to make yourself better than God created you to be." Or he plays to your ego: "Look at you. You look so spiritual with all your works that God has finally taken notice. You've earned His attention." The spirit of religion influences people to become manipulative and controlling to win God's approval. When people accept Jesus as their Savior, they change spiritual kingdoms. They move from Satan's kingdom to God's kingdom. But do they realize they have to change relational systems also? The tendency is to drag the legalistic structure from the world into the church and think that's how God's kingdom operates.

The spirit of religion will turn the lights off in your heart and shut down your authority. It will try to persuade you to believe you aren't good or pleasing enough to the Lord to possess any authority. That's why Paul told the

Galatian believers, "I do not set aside the grace of God; for if righteousness comes through the law, then Christ died in vain" (Gal. 2:21).

2. NATURAL CIRCUMSTANCES

There are all kinds of opposing circumstances in life because we live in a fallen, sinful world. Difficulties happen that are out of our control, and life doesn't always go our way. There are unexpected sicknesses, financial problems, relational difficulties—you name it. From the moment we wake up in the morning, life is coming at us full speed. It's a stressful world we live in these days, and that stress affects us. You can't even get in your car and drive to work without having to deal with traffic and the feelings it provokes.

All these circumstances speak to us. They have a voice whether we realize it or not. They're telling us things like, "Your prayers aren't working," or, "This pain means you're not going to be healed," or, "That person is angry with you, and the relationship can never be mended." Circumstances often speak doubt to your mind, and Satan will make sure their messages try to rob you of your sense of authority.

One fruit of the Spirit listed in Galatians 5:22–23 is longsuffering, or patience. This spiritual grace strengthens us as we stand in faith and endure opposition. It applies when dealing with both circumstances and people. We must be able to identify the messages being sent to us this way so we can reject any deceptions. After all, they are only circumstantial evidence. Even our natural judicial system won't accept circumstantial evidence to convict a defendant. The Lord expects us to stand in faith and reject voices and imaginations that threaten our spiritual authority.

3. CONDEMNATION

Satan is a master at bringing up your past and throwing it back in your face. He'll take your past sins, wrong attitudes, and strife-filled words and hammer your heart with them. He'll especially use those things that have been forgiven and cleansed by the blood of Jesus. His purpose is to rob you of your authority by triggering false guilt and shame so your heart will accept the judgment against you. Condemnation is what I call demonic glue. The Bible says, "A curse without cause shall not alight" (Prov. 26:2). Satan doesn't have the right or ability to simply overpower with a "curse" of sin, weakness, or failure. So he tricks you instead. If he can get you to accept condemnation, then you might also receive the assumed punishment that goes with it. Once unworthiness enters your mind, his attacks against you begin to stick.

So resist condemnation at all costs. Like fear, condemnation is not from the Lord. He has given us a spirit of power and love and of a sound mind (2 Tim. 1:7). Yes, the Holy Spirit will convict us when necessary, but He doesn't use the devil to do it. God speaks to us by His grace and teaches us through the Word. The enemy condemns, and it's important to know the difference between the enemy's tactic and conviction from the Holy Spirit. Conviction corrects your attitude and behavior while reinforcing your faith and authority. Condemnation uses your bad attitude and behavior to disqualify you, your faith, and your authority.

4. Emotions

Having human emotions is normal. Our emotions are from God. He's the One who gave them to us. What's more, God has the same emotions we do. Jesus felt love, joy, pain, and everything in between; He even experienced fear and anxiety when He walked the earth, to the point that He sweat drops of blood. However, mankind's sin in the Garden of Eden touched every aspect of our being, including our emotions. How we handle our emotions is what determines whether they are assets or liabilities at any given moment.

When the Lord took me to the third heaven for the first time, I learned a valuable lesson concerning my emotions. As I stood before His throne, the first thing I felt was a complete absence of fear, intimidation, condemnation, shame, guilt, disapproval, inadequacy, failure, and self-doubt. It was as if my emotions had been redeemed from earthly persuasions while I was in heaven. I felt unconditional love, acceptance, and value from the Lord. I was still the same person. I hadn't changed, but my feelings changed. Being guided by negative emotions and not what God says about us in His Word is very destructive to our Christian walk here on earth. The enemy twists our emotions to rob us of our authority.

5. Stealing the Revelation of Who We Are in Christ

The Word of God is the truth, and it alone defines who we are as new creations in Christ. Our feelings have nothing to do with it. Satan desperately wants to keep us from understanding and walking in God's Word. But it's our adherence to Scripture that enhances our authority. James calls it being doers of the Word: "But be doers of the word, and not hearers only, deceiving yourselves" (Jas. 1:22).

When I was in heaven standing before the throne, my heart cried out to Jesus, "Is this who You created us to be? Is this what it feels like to be a new creation in Christ Jesus?" In that moment, all the second-heaven hooks—fear, condemnation, inadequacy, and self-doubt—were removed. In total amazement, I felt the fullness of having been transformed into a new person. I was more than a new person; I was a new creation, able to see myself as the Lord sees me.

But when the encounter was over, I had to start dealing with my emotions about earthly situations all over again. Now, however, I had a tool from the experience, a memory of what it was like in heaven. Jesus had to struggle with His feelings about earthly situations also, but He resisted their pressure to overtake Him. He submitted to the Father and His Word, just as we must do. Jesus showed us the way by choosing to believe who the Father said He was. He approached His ministry, death, and resurrection in total faith. Nothing in this world corroborated His identity. Now He is seated at the right hand of the Father, and we are seated there with Him.

The second thing that happened to me in heaven pertained to authority. The Holy Spirit spun me around and showed me a portal in the floor. As I looked down, I saw the demonic spirits in the atmosphere over the city where the prayer meeting was being held. Hanging in the atmosphere were lower-level demons and a larger general that was giving them orders.

The Lord commanded me, "Launch your warfare from

here." The success of the warfare needed to come out of a solid understanding of who I was as a believer. In that revelation, authority welled up in me. It was as if I wore the authority as a cloak or as armor. The devil knows that if we walk in authority, we'll clean his clock. That's why he fights so hard against us in certain areas. We mustn't let the devil steal the revelation of who we are in Christ.

So the next time the enemy uses his tactics to say, "By what authority do you do these things?" just say, "By the authority Jesus has given me in His name. Get behind me, Satan. I will not doubt nor back down. I will stand and believe, and I'll watch heaven and earth be moved because of my faith."

Being bold and decisive is an act of love, and love is one of the greatest empowerments in the kingdom. Sometimes the enemy influences our relationships—family, friends, and others—to get us off balance. Our flesh and mind weren't created to handle every situation by themselves. The human spirit was meant to rule over the mind and the flesh. Paul told us in Romans 5:5, "The love of God has been poured out in our hearts by the Holy Spirit who was given to us." It's a spiritual thing. God's love in our hearts always leads us in the ways of the Holy Spirit. "Walk in the Spirit," Paul wrote, "and you shall not fulfill the lust of the flesh" (Gal. 5:16). We have to lean into the Spirit of God and His love to deal wisely with others.

CHAPTER 8

HOSTING GOD'S PRESENCE

HOSTING GOD'S GLORY, practicing the presence of God, waiting on the Lord, having times of refreshing in the Holy Spirit—these phrases are frequently used interchangeably, but they all represent the magnificence of experiencing the presence of God. David wrote, "In Your presence is fullness of joy" (Ps. 16:11, MEV). When a person is experiencing the fullness of joy in God's manifest presence, there's an explosion of intimacy, revelation, power, and spiritual authority. Sometimes that explosion is loud. Other times it's an explosion of quiet confidence and being overwhelmed with God's supernatural peace. All these manifestations are wrapped up in the blanket of joy.

We live in a world where natural circumstances and physical needs often scream for our attention like toddlers in their terrible twos. In an attempt to quiet those screams, it's easy to resort to our own power, wisdom, and resources, even our own authority. God has a better way. The way He has designed for us to walk in third-heaven authority is through intimacy with Him. In fact, there's a direct correlation between walking in the presence of God and the amount of third-heaven authority we are able to demonstrate.

God's glory manifests more readily where it is wanted and sought. Psalm 42:1–2 describes the hunger God desires us to have for Him: "As the deer pants for the water brooks, so pants my soul for You, O God. My soul thirsts for God, for the living God. When shall I come and appear before God?" Commentators agree that the deer presented here has been on the run from hunters in the wilderness. It is dry, thirsty, and worn out, longing for strength and refreshment. The deer knows where its answer lies: in the invigorating, cool water of a nearby brook. When it arrives there, the deer laps up the water. This is how God wants us to seek after Him, and when we are in the presence of Jesus, we experience the same strength and refreshment as the deer in the psalm.

In Western church culture, it's easy to assume a position where we treat being in relationship with Jesus as a cerebral exercise. We place so much value on intellectualism and being rational that we often overlook the emotional, passionate side of being with Jesus. I know because I had to walk through this learning process myself. The more I learned about the prophetic gifting God had placed upon my life, the more I realized I had to develop a relationship with Jesus and the Holy Spirit that was personal and intimate. It was out of that position of intimacy that I began to see true power and revelation in my life. The word *intimacy* scares so many believers because they don't know how to walk in it. They understand programs and religious ritual, but not intimacy. In their interpersonal relationships, they build walls around their heart and don't want to become vulnerable by exposing their emotional and passionate side. But in Jesus Christ, we must.

Paul told the Romans that the kingdom of God is not eating or drinking but righteousness, peace, and joy in the Holy Spirit (Rom. 14:17). Two of the three words he used to describe the kingdom of God were emotional states. Only one of the three words pointed to a relational position and the behavior connected to it. If that's how Paul viewed the kingdom of God, then we must take heed. Only by getting close to the Lord will you get the strength, revelation, and insight to be who God created you to be and do what He has called you to do.

Some have called this quest to move into a deeper place of intimacy with Him "practicing the presence of God," meaning to experience God's glory, His manifest presence. God's glory is His presence and the effect that presence has on us.

Practicing the presence of God is learning how to be in a place of intimacy with Him. Some have called it "building an atmosphere for the Holy Spirit," because the Holy Spirit works best in an atmosphere of intimacy. The Spirit releases His life-changing wisdom and power into our lives in that holy environment. Others have referred to it as "hosting the glory," the emphasis being on our personal responsibility to act as willing hosts and show God perpetual hospitality.

Isaiah 40:31 says, "Those who wait upon the LORD shall renew their strength" (MEV). Yet another description is "waiting on the Lord." That waiting is a time of serving Him with heartfelt reverence, where we only want to be with Him. Another phrase we see is "times of refreshing." Acts 3:19 says, "So that times of refreshing may come from the presence of the Lord." All these terms talk about the same experience but look at it from different angles, like the different facets of a precious diamond.

It is my belief that if I had not learned how to host the glory of God and develop my intimacy with Him, I would never have made it as far as I have. I would not be walking in third-heaven authority. I would not have experienced dreams and visions to the extent I have. Those things are directly proportional to the amount of intimacy I have developed, not only with Jesus but also with the Holy Spirit. I learned to trust Him and let Him take me beyond an intellectual relationship with God. At the heart level, I tapped into my own passions and felt the passions of the Holy Spirit as He worked within me.

Yet many people are afraid of being passionate with God. They simply don't know how, or they are afraid of being vulnerable and getting hurt. Some just shut down their hearts, thinking that is the best way to overcome negative emotions such as fear, condemnation, or inadequacy. The positive feelings, however, are squelched and buried with the negative ones.

When we allow ourselves to feel the positive emotions God has given us, it drastically increases the revelation we receive from the Holy Spirit. Only half the revelation the Holy Spirit gives us is actually connected to the intellectual, rational part of the message. This is true whether it comes through the written Word of God, visions, dreams, angelic encounters, or the gifts of the Spirit. The other half of the revelation has to do with the feelings and perceptions that come with it. When I teach people how to interpret encounters with God, I not only address what was seen and heard but also the feelings and unspoken perceptions they had at the time. The whole of the experience is important.

INTIMACY AND AUTHORITY

Examples of this intimacy and how it relates to authority can be found in Scripture. The two best examples, in my opinion, are two shepherd kings: King David in the Old Testament and King Jesus in the New Testament. They both wore their authority in a way that changed the lives of everyone around them. They understood that authority required submission to God as well as being responsible for those who were under their care. They also understood that success could not be achieved without intimacy with God.

The shepherd kings David and Jesus were both worshipping warriors who embodied tenderness and militancy, kindness and power. Militancy without the tenderness born of intimacy will burn you out and cause you to run over others and become abusive. We'll become weary in well-doing and lose our passion.

King Jesus brought God's kingdom in power, but the people felt greatly loved by Him. King David was a great warrior, and out of his psalmist's heart flowed anointed music and passionate worship.

In 2 Samuel 6, when David removed his kingly garments to dance before the Lord in a linen ephod, he wasn't removing his authority; he was disclosing the intimate priestly garments worn underneath them. His wife, Michal, was embittered because he would dare remove his kingly garments in public. Michal assumed David's subjects would think less of him, but she failed to see he was actually exalting God and being a true example to his subjects.

I'm reminded of a vision the Lord gave me many years ago. I'd been praying in the Spirit for quite some time when the Holy Spirit drew me into the spirit realm and a vision unfolded before me. The setting was a castle like those in medieval Europe. It was clean and bright. In the tower of the castle was the king's bedroom. He was a good king, and the people loved him. One morning as he was getting dressed and ready to face the day, he heard a commotion outside the castle walls. An enemy army had assembled and was preparing to lay siege to the castle. The good king and his subjects within the castle were dressed in white apparel that shone like light. The enemy outside the walls wore black apparel and armor.

The enemy king rode up to the castle and issued a challenge to the good king. He said, "There's no need for all the bloodshed. Let us battle—king against king, man against man. Whoever wins receives the spoils and the allegiance of all the people." The good king quickly accepted the challenge and then went into his armor room. The armor bearer attended him and put all the armor and weaponry over the king's bare skin; then the king was led to his stallion, which he rode out the castle gate to meet the enemy. Well-trained in battle, the king knew what to do, yet as he engaged in combat, the armor began to scrape his skin. The pain distracted him, and he began to hesitate in some of his moves. Ultimately the evil king won, not because he was a better warrior but because the good king's armor chafed his skin.

It was an unusual vision, and I wondered what it could mean. Then I heard the booming voice of the Lord say, "The failure of the good king was in not putting on his *undergarments*. If he had put on undergarments before donning his armor and weapons, he would have been victorious. His skill was greater than that of the enemy king."

Then the Lord said this to me: "The undergarments are the garments of praise and worship, which create intimacy with Me." My mind was quickened to the verse where the Lord said He was giving His people "the garment of praise for the spirit of heaviness" (Isa. 61:3). He continued, "Spend time with Me daily in worship and praise so you will learn My voice. It will become the protection that keeps the spiritual armor from becoming burdensome, cutting into your skin, and distracting you during warfare. Intimacy and combat skills go hand in hand. If you want to defeat the enemy at every hand, then develop a close relationship with My Spirit. That will undergird the *authority* I have given to you."

As you can imagine, I was overcome with awe.

King Jesus demonstrated these dynamics when He walked the earth. He purposely got alone with the Father and spent time with Him. He learned how to be sensitive to the Holy Spirit. King Jesus listened for the words of the Father and then released them to the people. He watched the works of the Father in the Spirit and then did those works among the people. As ministers, CK and I learned early on that we needed to develop a ministry mindset based on prayer and intimacy with God. First, we would bring the people to God in prayer. Second, we would bring God to the people through ministry. All believers can do the same. Ministry flows out of intimacy with God. Ministry has greater success when we make it a lifestyle to value and build a close relationship with God.

King Jesus confirmed this point in His interaction with Lazarus' sisters, Mary and Martha. "Now it happened as they went that He entered a certain village; and a certain woman named Martha welcomed Him into her house. And she had a sister called Mary, who also sat at Jesus' feet and heard His word" (Luke 10:38–39).

Tension arose between Martha and Mary: "But Martha

was distracted with much serving, and she approached Him and said, 'Lord, do You not care that my sister has left me to serve alone? Therefore tell her to help me.' And Jesus answered and said to her, 'Martha, Martha, you are worried and troubled about many things. But one thing is needed, and Mary has chosen that good part, which will not be taken away from her'" (Luke 10:40–42).

Certain tasks had to be done. They just were not as weighty as sitting at Jesus' feet. We need to take care of business, but not at the expense of spending time with God. Mary chose the one thing that was needful: developing a close relationship with her Lord. We find another story in the seventh chapter of Luke. A woman in the city whom the Pharisees labeled a sinner washed Jesus' feet with her tears and wiped them with her hair. Then she anointed His feet with costly oil, all because she loved Jesus. Like the deer panting for the water, these two women valued their time with the Lord above everything else.

Intimacy With the Bridegroom

In both the Old and New Testaments, God describes Himself as a husband and the church as His bride, a distinction that's not about gender but about intimacy and position. One such passage is Hosea 2:14–16:

> "Therefore, behold, I will allure her, will bring her
> into the wilderness, and speak comfort to her. I will
> give her her vineyards from there, and the Valley
> of Achor as a door of hope; she shall sing there, as
> in the days of her youth, as in the day when she
> came up from the land of Egypt. And it shall be, in

that day," says the LORD, "that you will call Me 'My Husband,' and no longer call Me 'My Master.'"

God sincerely desires for us to come to the point where we call Him "my Husband," not "my Master." The pressure of fulfilling the tasks at hand will keep us in a place where we see Jesus only as our Master. However, we will begin to see Him as "my Husband" when we spend intimate time with Him.

There are many other passages that reveal God's longing for closeness with us. Song of Solomon 5:16 paints a picture of Jesus' passion for His bride: "Yes, he is altogether lovely. This is my beloved, and this is my friend." Ezekiel 16:8 carries the same analogy: "'When I passed by you again and looked upon you, indeed your time was the time of love; so I spread My wing over you and covered your nakedness. Yes, I swore an oath to you and entered into a covenant with you, and you became Mine,' says the Lord GOD."

In Matthew 25, Jesus gives us the parable of the ten virgins, in which the bride represents the church and the bridegroom represents Him. Ephesians 5:25 says, "Husbands, love your wives, just as Christ also loved the church and gave Himself for her." There is no more intimate relationship than that of a husband and wife.

One of the steepest learning curves I ever experienced came the year CK and I were married. I knew I loved her and wanted to spend the rest of my life with her, but I had to learn how to live with her as a husband. It's one thing to tell your wife you love her and genuinely feel it in your heart. It's quite another thing to open to her the deepest longings of your heart and share your most personal dreams. Then to learn how to connect with who she is as a godly woman with her own visions and dreams, I had to learn to become one with my wife and develop the kind of closeness that would nurture her as a woman. The unexpected reward was that I too was nurtured, and I became much more confident in my own masculinity.

That same year, CK and I both received the baptism in the Holy Spirit. Suddenly, I was thrust into doing the same thing with the Lord. I had accepted Jesus as my Savior years prior, but the baptism of the Holy Spirit brought me into unparalleled intimacy with Him. I thought I loved Jesus before, and I did. Now, however, I fell "in" love with Him. Basically, as I learned to open my heart to my wife and to the Lord, I discovered there was strength in vulnerability. I had to learn to trust them enough to let them see me as I actually was, flaws and all, and know they would never intentionally hurt me.

As I spent time with my wife, I discovered how to communicate my affection for her, and the same thing happened in my relationship with Jesus. It also became normal for me to show my wife affection in public without caring about what people thought. I would hold her hand when we walked through the shopping mall and give her a hug or kiss. The same thing happened with Jesus. I now raise my hands and sing songs of love to Him, worshipping Him. I've learned to discard my pride so I can host the presence of God. Pride and embarrassment are hindrances to experiencing the true power of God.

In my relationships with God and my wife, I found that the only way to become bold enough to manifest my love for them publicly was to practice it at home. I began to simply wait upon God in my prayer closet and allow the

Holy Spirit's anointing to come. As I did, His presence would consume me, and songs and prayers would burst out of me. On many occasions I would laugh, cry, and dance before the Lord. As this intimacy grew, I found myself displaying my feelings in public without embarrassment. It seemed to just happen. The power of God increased dramatically in my life too! I saw an increase in the gifts and fruit of the Spirit, as well as signs, wonders, miracles, visions, dreams, and angelic visitations. The more intimate Jesus and I became, the more of Him I craved. The manifestations of the Spirit and power of God in my life were byproducts of my relationship with Him.

If you really want to host the glory of God and see it manifest in your life, there are two things you must do. First, you have to contend for it because your flesh isn't used to God's power operating in your life and will try to keep that from happening. You can only break free of strongholds when you yield to the Spirit. You have to make a quality decision that you're not going to live the way you had been living any longer. You must decide that nothing is more important than pursuing God's presence—nothing. Then set aside time to seek the Lord and His Spirit. You have to need Him and want His glory in your life.

Second, you must choose to make every decision and approach every action with His presence in mind. Once the glory has come, you never want it to lift. Never take God's presence for granted or ignore it. The Holy Spirit has feelings, and He can be quenched. Let Him lead and empower you out of a place of intimacy. If you do, He will fill you with wisdom to make godly decisions and release the kingdom of heaven in your life and in the lives of those around you. And your awareness of your spiritual authority will increase.

CHAPTER 9

THE ONE KEY TO WALKING IN AUTHORITY

B E ANXIOUS FOR nothing," Paul urged, "but in *every-thing* by prayer...let your requests be made known to God" (Phil. 4:6, emphasis added). Everything—our whole lives, all that we do—should be driven by prayer. As simple as it may sound, prayer is the primary key to walking in our full authority. It calls upon the spiritual realm to invade the natural realm. I like the way renowned healing evangelist Smith Wigglesworth put it when asked about the importance of prayer. "Well," he said, "I don't ever pray any longer than twenty minutes."

"What?" his questioner exclaimed. After pausing a moment, Wigglesworth continued, "Yes, but I never go twenty minutes without praying."[1] Prayer wasn't a now-and-then act for Smith Wigglesworth; it was the backbone of his life, and the same must be true for us.

Prayer is the backbone of the church, the ecclesia of the Lord. God's chosen method of intervention is prayer. God works through people. For various reasons, it's the way He has set things up. Whether we or others are praying, prayer moves the heart of God and changes situations.

Ephesians 6:18 tells us, "Pray at all times (on every occasion, in every season) in the Spirit, with all [manner of] prayer and entreaty" (AMPC). Here Paul uses the phrase "all manner." That simply means there are different types of prayer for different situations and results. This chapter explores those types of prayer and shows why it is critical for us to know the differences and apply them. But first, what is prayer, really?

Ultimately, prayer is communicating in the spiritual realm with all three members of the Godhead—God the Father, God the Son, and God the Holy Spirit. Prayer is not a monologue; it's a dialogue through which we express our hearts and listen to His. God is a dialogical God, and He desires our fellowship. Prayer is not meant to be an information bureau whereby He learns of our problems and fixes them. He already knows our needs before we even speak. Yet because He loves us, loves faith, and desires a relationship with us, He says, "Go ahead and tell Me what you need."

Like a doting father or grandfather, God loves it when we come to Him. Grandparents in particular buy all kinds of goodies for their grandkids, and when they visit, the grandkids head straight to the pantry or fridge and open it with full authority to get what's inside. They know whose they are. If the kids didn't take what had been provided for them, the grandparents would be disappointed. It brings them great joy to see their kids taking advantage of their provision. The same is true with our heavenly Father. He delights in giving good things to His children and wants us to use the authority that is rightfully ours. Those rights are not for just any kids, only family.

Most of us are familiar with Matthew 7:11, "If you then, being evil, know how to give good gifts to your children, how much more will your Father who is in heaven give good things to those who ask Him!" That's true. And what the Father really loves is when His kids simply crawl up in His lap and visit, sharing their hearts and getting hugs. That's what intimate prayer is all about. It's about spending time in the Father's embrace.

Faith absolutely thrills God, and true prayer is about faith. It's knowing when you are talking to Him that He's listening and responding, even when you don't see it. Jesus demonstrated how prayer helps us drive away doubt and overcome temptation and enhances our spiritual perception, giving us the ability to escape calamities. The nineteenth-century preacher Charles Spurgeon wrote that prayer is "doubt's destroyer, ruin's remedy, the antidote to all anxieties."[2] When Jesus cursed the fig tree and it died, His disciples were astounded. Jesus told them in essence, "Have faith in God, and you can do the same thing." (See Mark 11:22–24.) God operates in faith. Jesus operates in faith and prayer. So dialoguing with the Lord is vital. Yet it should be a natural thing, where we just pour our hearts out to God and then listen.

There's also an aspect of prayer where we submit to God. "Therefore submit to God," James wrote. "Resist the devil and he will flee from you" (Jas. 4:7). Part of submitting ourselves to God is developing this prayer life and realizing we have the authority to resist the devil. Prayer involves actually using the authority Jesus has given us to rebuke and resist the devil so he will flee from us. We will explore this more a little later.

The success or failure of every God-inspired endeavor is based on prayer. Every move of God in a person's life, as well as every revival in the entire history of the church, has come through prayer. When observing the life of Jesus, we see His regular routine was spending time alone with the Father. Then, out of that fellowship time He would be empowered to minister to those around Him as well as accomplish the tasks to which He was called. Jesus showed us that communing with the Father is not just a worthwhile endeavor but a necessity.

The bottom line is that prayer and studying God's Word are the two most important elements to having a fruitful Christian life. It sounds like a no-brainer, and it is. Yet even though Christians know it, most don't practice it. I echo Peter when he said, "Therefore I intend always to remind you of these qualities, though you know them and are established in the truth that you have" (2 Pet. 1:12, ESV). More than anything else, the enemy attempts to stop Christians from engaging in those two disciplines, prayer and study of the Word, because that is where we find authority and empowerment. This chapter is focusing on the element of prayer. More often than not, it takes resisting the devil and fighting off distractions to enter into communion with God.

As we noted earlier, Paul mentioned "all manner," or different forms, of prayer. Each of these forms operates by different rules, and it's to our advantage to know and implement all of them. In this chapter we will look at seven different types of New Testament prayer, each with its own key distinction.

1. THE PRAYER OF PETITION AND SUPPLICATION

As the definition indicates, this kind of prayer is a formal request to God to meet a specific need. First John 5:14–15 tells us: "Now this is the confidence that we have in Him, that if we ask anything according to His will, He hears us. And if we know that He hears us, whatever we ask, we know that we have the petitions that we have asked of Him." This speaks of specific requests, but what we seek must be according to His will.

To ask according to His will, we have to find what we're seeking in God's Word. We need to find out what the Bible says about our request, and then we ask the Holy Spirit how to take that biblical principle and apply it to the specific situation in our lives. When we do that, we're praying according to God's will, and we can have the assurance that those petitions are answered.

God loves His children tenderly and cares about what's going on in our lives. He wants us to pray in a way that He can answer. Paul instructed, "Be anxious for nothing, but in everything by prayer and supplication, with thanksgiving, let your requests be made known to God; and the peace of God, which surpasses all understanding, will guard your hearts and minds through Christ Jesus" (Phil. 4:6–7). We already saw where Paul said for us to do "everything by prayer." He continued by adding "supplication." Prayer and supplication are closely connected, but they are different. Prayer involves many aspects of dialoguing with God, while supplication is a matter of naming our request specifically and contending for it expectantly until it comes to pass.

2. THE PRAYER OF THANKSGIVING AND PRAISE

In Philippians 4:6, Paul says we must do everything by "prayer and supplication, *with thanksgiving*" (emphasis added). We tend to read right past those two words, but they are vital to our prayer experience. Thanksgiving is a way of expressing worship, not only thanking God for who He is, which is a primary thing we must do, but also thanking Him for what He has done and is doing for us. What's important to grasp here is that giving thanks and praise in prayer is actually a deep expression of faith. This kind of worship is like saying, "God, regardless of what I see, regardless of my circumstances, You are God. I am not. I trust You. I praise You." It's when we do as Paul and Silas did in Acts 16 after they had been beaten and locked in the innermost dungeon. Though their feet were in stocks, they sang praises to God with no idea what their future held. They knew only who held their future, and He miraculously delivered them.

Praising God in prayer when life doesn't make sense and we don't understand doesn't minimize or deny what we are going through. Instead, it redirects our focus to who God is. We are giving thanks to God for responding to the prayer we are currently offering up. We are thanking Him for the answer and for moving in our lives, for delivering, healing, and restoring us. Whatever petition we're giving to Him, we thank God that He hears and cares for us, and then we worship Him for bringing the desired outcome. That is one of the strongest prayers of faith that can be prayed.

Sometimes before I even voice my petition, I'll enter a state of worship and praise, where I thank and glorify God before I even tell Him what I have need of. Other times, as acts of faith, I'll spend the whole time worshipping God, thanking and praising Him for how He's moving in my life and giving me wisdom and direction to navigate the situations I'm facing.

3. THE PRAYER OF BINDING AND LOOSING

When we bind and loose in prayer, we use our spiritual authority to counter the works and strategies of Satan and release the works and plans of Jesus into the situation. We resist hell and release heaven. This type of prayer is spoken of in Matthew 16:18–19, where Jesus said: "And I also say to you that you are Peter, and on this rock I will build My church, and the gates of Hades shall not prevail against it. And I will give you the keys of the kingdom of heaven, and whatever you bind on earth will be bound in heaven, and whatever you loose on earth will be loosed in heaven."

The word *loose* means to unlock or to declare lawful, to release those things that have already been unlocked and declared lawful in heaven. In this passage, Jesus was saying the authority given to the Sanhedrin under the old covenant had been transferred to the New Testament church, the ecclesia, the body of believers under the new covenant. As Christ's representatives from heaven, the church has the delegated authority from Jesus Himself to bind on earth what is bound in heaven. That means we have the authority to lock or to declare unlawful the things that are locked up and declared unlawful in heaven. This authority is ours because Jesus defeated the enemy on the cross and now has been raised up and is seated at the right hand of the Father in heaven. We now stand on the earth as the enforcers of the plans and purposes of heaven.

One reason this prayer is interesting is that we typically think of prayer as talking to God. But binding and loosing involves speaking to the enemy too. We rebuke him by using our authority. Yet it all starts with James 4:7,

"Therefore submit to God." A lack of submission and obedience nullifies our authority.

Jesus effectively demonstrated this prayer when He raised Lazarus from the dead in John 11. When Jesus stood before the tomb, He lifted His eyes to heaven and said, "Father, I thank You that You have heard Me" (v. 41). Talking to God like that is a form of prayer most of us are accustomed to. But then Jesus turned and spoke to Lazarus, crying with a loud voice, "Lazarus, come forth!" (v. 43). He wasn't speaking to God; He was issuing the command of faith.

On another occasion, Jesus took authority over the demonic influences that were coming against Peter when He said, "Get behind Me, Satan!" (Matt. 16:23). This prayer is demonstrated throughout the New Testament when Jesus cast out demons, raised the dead, healed the sick, and turned water into wine. The gifts of the Spirit and the miraculous are demonstrated through this prayer. Like Jesus and the first-century believers, we have the authority to speak to the problem itself and declare the answer. In Mark 11, Jesus didn't tell the fig tree that it was a problem or in His way. He spoke to it and said, "Let no one eat fruit from you ever again" (v. 14). He declared what the end would be. We have that same authority as believers.

4. THE PRAYER OF AGREEMENT

This type of prayer is where two or more believers pray together for the same outcome. Jesus said, "Assuredly, I say to you, whatever you bind on earth will be bound in heaven, and whatever you loose on earth will be loosed in heaven. Again I say to you that if two of you agree on earth concerning anything that they ask, it will be done for them by My Father in heaven" (Matt. 18:18–19). Whenever Jesus says "assuredly," He's saying, "Hey, guys, listen up! This is important. I don't want you to miss this."

Prayer is even more effective when there are multiple people storming heaven. But when other people are involved, there must be accord; otherwise, everyone is praying their own notions in different ways. To see maximum impact, it must be clear exactly what the group will be praying for and what the answer should be. Then you pray together in agreement for that purpose. This is a strong prayer spiritually because the Bible says one can put a thousand to flight and two can put ten thousand to flight (Deut. 32:30). There's an exponential increase in the display of God's power when believers pray in agreement.

5. The Prayer of Intercession

Paul said: "Therefore I exhort first of all that supplications, prayers, intercessions, and giving of thanks be made for all men for kings and all who are in authority, that we may lead a quiet and peaceable life in all godliness and reverence. For this is good and acceptable in the sight of God our Savior" (1 Tim. 2:1–3). In this passage, Paul mentions several kinds of prayer. One of them is intercession.

Intercessory prayer is going before the Lord on behalf of someone or something else—another person or a city, nation, or cause. At its core, intercession is when we go to the Lord for the needs of others. The Holy Spirit will use us not only to come into agreement with others but to bind the enemy off their lives and war in the spirit on their behalf. Through intercession we can stand in the gap against the spiritual forces that are assaulting them and break strongholds to help free them. Intercessory prayer is going to the Father on behalf of someone else and asking Him to supply heavenly bread to meet the person's needs.

6. THE PRAYER FOR DEDICATION AND DIRECTION

This prayer is asking God for wisdom and direction when you don't already know His will. This is the only prayer in Scripture in which we are told to pray, "If it be Your will." James 4:13–15 says:

> Come now, you who say, "Today or tomorrow we will go to such and such a city, spend a year there, buy and sell, and make a profit"; whereas you do not know what will happen tomorrow. For what is your life? It is even a vapor that appears for a little time and then vanishes away. Instead you ought to say, "If the Lord wills, we shall live and do this or that."

Many people think we're supposed to pray "if it be Your will" whenever we pray, but that is not scriptural. Think about it. If you're praying for someone's salvation, you don't pray, "If it be Your will." The Bible says God "desires all men to be saved and to come to the knowledge of the truth" (1 Tim. 2:4, MEV). It's always God's will for somebody to be saved. The same is true when it comes to healing. You don't have to ask what God's will is. James wrote:

> Is anyone among you sick? He should call in the church elders (the spiritual guides). And they should

> pray over him, anointing him with oil in the Lord's
> name. And the prayer [that is] of faith will save him
> who is sick, and the Lord will restore him; and if he
> has committed sins, he will be forgiven.
>
> —JAMES 5:14–15, AMPC

Praying "if it be Your will" when God's will is laid out plain in Scripture is a manifestation of doubt and unbelief. Neither Jesus nor His disciples walked up to a blind person and said, "Father, if it be Your will, would You please heal this person?" No. They knew what the Father's will was and commanded, "Eyes, be opened. Be healed, in Jesus' name!"

Yet in times when we need personal direction and clarity, praying "if it be Your will" is absolutely God's will. Pressing forward in life according to our own agendas and plans and not following His leading is not only prideful; it's foolish. "Be very careful, then, how you live—not as unwise but as wise, making the most of every opportunity, because the days are evil. Therefore do not be foolish, but understand what the Lord's will is" (Eph. 5:15–17, NIV).

7. PRAYER IN THE SPIRIT (TONGUES)

In 1 Corinthians 14, Paul said, "For he who speaks in a tongue does not speak to men but to God" (v. 2). That is powerful. When you are praying in tongues, you are bypassing men, even yourself, and going straight to the Godhead. Have you ever heard the phrase, "I have to get out of my own head"? Praying in tongues does that. Paul continues verse 2 saying, "for no one understands him; however, in the spirit he speaks mysteries." Then he says in verse 14, "For if I pray in a tongue, my spirit prays, but my understanding is unfruitful."

Tongues is a heavenly language that is provided by the Holy Spirit—our prayer language. It's not something learned with your intellect, and it doesn't make sense in the natural mind. God designed it that way because praying in tongues requires faith and humility. When praying in tongues, you are naturally saying, "I want more of You, God; more of You, Holy Spirit; and less of myself. I am yielding my own mind and will to You." All the prayer types can be prayed in tongues, and it is such an important prayer tool, we will discuss it further in the next chapter.

It's important to note that in 1 Corinthians 14, Paul also talks about the charismatic gift of tongues, which is giving a message in tongues in a public assembly. This is different from praying in our personal prayer language, as it must be accompanied by the interpretation. Speaking in tongues in an assembly is God speaking through us to the people gathered, but praying in the tongues of our heavenly prayer language is us speaking to God, and He knows exactly what we are saying, even though we don't.

When we use the seven types of prayers discussed in this chapter, our obligation is to pray in faith in the name of Jesus. It's God's obligation to answer. We can't make anything happen in our strength, but we can release the authority that is ours through Jesus' name so God can move in on the scene and bring the power of heaven.

CHAPTER 10

HOW TO KEEP YOUR FAITH STRONG

Did you know God gave you a powerful prayer key to overcome discouragement, weariness, and the things that try to drain us? When Jesus said, "I will not leave you comfortless" (John 14:18, KJV), He meant it! There's a powerful way to pray God's will into your life with authority. I'm talking, of course, about praying in the Spirit, specifically in tongues. In the last chapter we looked at the different types of prayer, and we touched on tongues. In this chapter we are going to dig a little deeper and find some golden nuggets that will revolutionize your prayer life.

Paul said in 1 Corinthians 14:2, "For he who speaks in a tongue *does not speak to men but to God*" (emphasis added). This statement may seem like a small detail, but it's actually quite significant. Paul is not referring here to the charismatic gift of diverse tongues that is listed in 1 Corinthians 12. We know this because in 1 Corinthians 14:21 he clarifies that in the charismatic gift of tongues, God is speaking to man. So when a message is delivered in a public assembly in a different kind of tongue, it needs to be interpreted for the congregation to understand, because it is a message from God to man.

In 1 Corinthians 14:2, however, Paul says, "he who speaks in a tongue does not speak to men but to God." Here Paul is talking about a personal prayer language from the heavenlies that bypasses our intellect to hook us up directly with God and the ways of the Spirit. Paul goes on to say,

117

"...for no one understands him; however, in the spirit he speaks mysteries." These mysteries are revealed secrets and themes of the kingdom that cannot be discerned in any way other than through the Holy Spirit. When you pray in tongues, you speak mysteries. The Spirit is praying through you perfectly, even about things you may not be aware of. They are mysteries.

What's beautiful is all born-again believers have this ability. According to Ephesians 1:13, when people receive Jesus as their Lord and Savior, the Holy Spirit comes inside them. They can then be filled, or baptized, with the Holy Spirit and speak a perfect, fluent, heavenly prayer language. They don't have to spend five years studying the Scriptures, although they should endeavor to know God's Word. They don't have to learn the ins and outs of the Christian walk and how to mature in the body of Christ, although, again, they should. None of those things are necessary to begin praying in that wonderful heavenly language. As you exercise your new language, the Holy Spirit becomes your supernatural teacher. The Scriptures will come alive with new illumination. God will give revelation and insight concerning your individual life and the body of Christ on planet Earth. The Holy Spirit will reveal God's will and purposes and pray them through us for us.

Paul told the Romans, "So too the [Holy] Spirit comes to our aid and bears us up in our weakness; for we do not know what prayer to offer nor how to offer it worthily as we ought, but the Spirit Himself goes to meet our supplication and pleads in our behalf" (Rom. 8:26, AMPC). We do not know what to pray for or how to pray for everything. But the Spirit comes alongside us. He knows what to pray for and how to pray for it. He knows because He's God and He's the Spirit of God within our hearts. He knows the will of God for our lives. He knows our destiny. He knows the answer to every question that confronts us. He knows how to circumvent the circumstances in our lives. He knows how to remove the mountains. He knows all of it, and He has given us a tool: that we can slip into our heavenly prayer language and begin to pray and pray and pray in the Spirit.

I've noticed at times that I pray in the Spirit with zero sense of what I'm praying or feeling. It's then that I press through by faith, knowing that "my spirit prays, but my understanding is unfruitful" (1 Cor. 14:14). Then, usually sometime later, an hour or possibly even days later, I'll be going about my business and seemingly out of nowhere the Spirit will manifest, or I will be hit with unusual wisdom about certain situations or overwhelming peace or power. I'll think, "Wow. Where'd that come from?" And the Holy Spirit will whisper, "That's a result of praying in your prayer language when you didn't feel anything."

"But you, beloved," Jude wrote, "building yourselves up on your most holy faith, praying in the Holy Spirit, keep yourselves in the love of God, looking for the mercies of our Lord Jesus Christ unto eternal life" (Jude 20–21). Jude is talking about how to avoid being depleted by all the discouragers and things that drain our physical, mental, and spiritual energy. We are to build ourselves up. We are admonished in Galatians 6:9 to "not grow weary while doing good, for in due season we shall reap if we do not lose heart." The truth is, however, that we *do* sometimes grow weary, to the point that we enter a slumber, a callousness, and we don't perform at our peak level. The good news is that help is available.

There's a technique the Holy Spirit has placed within the church body that He Himself oversees. It allows us to be built up on our most holy faith and to "rise like an edifice higher and higher" (Jude 20, AMPC). This is the Spirit's way of recharging our spiritual batteries. And when your spiritual battery is recharged, the current overflows to the natural realm, recharging your physical batteries! Sometimes we can get exhausted in the natural, and it affects us spiritually. We are just physically tired and don't want to do anything, including praying or going to church. The enemy loves to attack us to the point of physical and spiritual exhaustion. Sometimes what we need is just to get some rest, and the Holy Spirit will help us do that.

Yet when we stop praying, reading the Word, and doing the other things daily that keep us spiritually nourished, our minds and physical bodies get depleted. Interestingly, this kind of exhaustion is different from the exhaustion we get from physical exertion. The fatigue that comes from spiritual malnourishment is an exhaustion of the heart. It makes us unable to face life's circumstances from a spiritual place. Instead of operating in the Spirit, we begin to operate in the flesh. The flesh can't accomplish spiritual things. It's possible to try to fulfill the things of God in the power of our flesh, but there's nothing more exhausting than that.

The way we build ourselves up and recharge our bodies and spirits is to pray in our heavenly prayer language, tongues. As I mentioned before, we can even use tongues when praying the seven kinds of prayers we discussed in the last chapter. For example, if you're interceding for a certain individual, you can call out the person's name to God while speaking in tongues. When you pray for the person in tongues, you can know for sure the Holy Spirit is assisting you to pray exactly what that person needs. Often we have no idea in our own minds how to pray for the individual. Anything you can pray in your natural language, you can do in tongues. Paul declared this to the Corinthians. You can sing in the Spirit and with your understanding. You can pray in the Spirit and with your understanding. You can give thanks in the Spirit and with your understanding.

When Paul uses the phrases "in the spirit," "my spirit prays," and "pray with the spirit" in 1 Corinthians 14, he is talking about tongues (vv. 2, 14–15). In fact, 1 Corinthians 14 could be labeled Paul's tongues chapter. So when Jude talks about "building yourselves up on your most holy faith, praying in the Holy Spirit" (Jude 20), we must conclude that praying in tongues plays a role. It doesn't accomplish 100 percent, but it accounts for a significant portion.

TONGUES AND THE ARMOR OF GOD

In Ephesians 6, Paul writes about the importance of believers putting on the whole armor of God:

> Finally, my brethren, be strong in the Lord and in the power of His might. Put on the whole armor of God, that you may be able to stand against the wiles of the devil. For we do not wrestle against flesh and blood, but against principalities, against powers, against the rulers of the darkness of this age, against spiritual hosts of wickedness in the heavenly places. Therefore take up the whole armor of God, that you may be able to withstand in the evil day, and having done all, to stand.

> Stand therefore, having girded your waist with truth, having put on the breastplate of righteousness, and having shod your feet with the preparation of the gospel of peace; above all, taking the shield of faith with which you will be able to quench all the fiery darts of the wicked one. And take the helmet of salvation, and the sword of the Spirit, which is the word of God.
>
> —EPHESIANS 6:10–17

Paul is addressing all believers in this passage. No one is exempt. There isn't a single believer who is so righteous, so perfect, or so sheltered that he or she is not subject to the attacks and influences of the enemy. Man's worldly system of thought is completely void of the revelation of God, and there's a very real spiritual war going on that's directed against the kingdom of God, which includes the King's children.

For this reason, Paul says in Ephesians 6:11 to "put on" and in verse 13 to "take up" the armor of God. We have to consider why he would tell us to do this if we were automatically wearing this armor when we were born again. To survive and thrive in our Christian pilgrimage, we must have the breastplate of righteousness and the helmet of salvation securely fastened. Yes, God gives them to us, but it's up to us to put them on.

Part of donning our spiritual armor is to accept and walk in the revelation of God in the areas of His truth, righteousness, peace, faith, salvation, and Word. That is how you put it on. When you do, it becomes impenetrable armor, and you dominate in it.

And why do we wear our spiritual armor? It's not to

sit down or take a nap. It's not to eat a big meal, watch a movie, or go to the ball game. We put on the armor of God to fight the good fight of faith in the arena of the mind. We may think the enemy is attacking our finances or our relationships, but the real battle is in the mind. We must keep our hearts and minds strong.

Once your armor is firmly secure, how do you wield it? Paul tells us: "praying always with all prayer and supplication *in the Spirit,* being watchful to this end with all perseverance and supplication for all the saints" (Eph. 6:18, emphasis added). The armor is used primarily in prayer, particularly when we pray in the Spirit.

PRAY AT ALL TIMES

We saw in the last chapter that Ephesians 6:18 tells us to *"pray at all times* (on every occasion, in every season) in the Spirit, *with all [manner of] prayer and entreaty"* (AMPC, emphasis added). Again, I want to be clear that praying "in the Spirit" includes praying in tongues as well as with your own learned language. Paul made this abundantly clear in his teaching to the Corinthians and other churches. Praying in the Spirit is critical because the Spirit searches the heart of God, His plans for our destiny, and who we are inside and out. As we pray in tongues, the Holy Spirit reveals those mysteries, those secrets, that edify and charge us up. Through this process we rise higher and higher in our spiritual knowledge, our wisdom, and our ability to allow God to use us to bring His kingdom.

Back in 1977 when our ministry was just beginning, CK and I were assistant pastors in Redding, California. It was only temporary, as we were helping another man establish a ministry. We understood that the Holy Spirit was maturing us to a place where He could lead us to our next assignment. Things were great; then these little dissatisfactions started popping up. Our hearts began to wander, looking for something new.

It's important to note that when there is uneasiness and dissatisfaction, it's possible that something is coming and you're getting ready for a change. When you feel that uneasiness, two things are necessary. First, begin praying in the Spirit and listen for the Lord's direction and timing; don't try to act on your own in the flesh. Second, be careful to not allow strife to come in. The enemy loves to come in the back door. He tries to stir up discord, bitterness, and offense between you and those around you.

It's important to keep in mind that just because God is moving you on to something else, it doesn't mean the current place and people are not wonderful. They deserve all the love, support, and ministry you can pour into them until the Holy Spirit says, "Now go."

During that season when we were assisting the minister in Redding, a prophet of God, who ordained CK and me, came to preach a meeting in our church. After the meeting, he came to our house for fellowship, and we had a nice visit. As he was leaving to return to his motel room, he stopped at our front door, looked us directly in the eyes, and said, "Pray yourself into the will of God." Then he turned around and left. We knew exactly what that meant. In those days, in order for this prophet to ordain someone, the person had to commit to praying in tongues for at least two hours daily. He wouldn't even bother with you if you didn't do that because he knew what it took to walk in a power-filled ministry. "Pray yourself into the will of God."

I will never forget those words because that's exactly what we did.

What's so neat about praying in tongues is that you don't have to know what you're praying about. The Holy Spirit is the One who does the work. It's your spirit that prays, as the apostle Paul said, but it is the Holy Spirit who gives the words or the unction. He's the motivator. And as it comes through us, we begin to pray ourselves into the will of God. We pray our family into the will of God. We pray our finances into the will of God. We pray our health into the will of God. We pray our ministries into the will of God. We pray our neighbors into the will of God.

Yes, they are free moral agents, but the principle in Scripture is that our prayers and intercession for our neighbors and those the Holy Spirit takes us into prayer about avail much. They have impact. The Holy Spirit through our prayers begins to reshape and to ward off negative influences and the things coming against their lives. Nobody in their right mind would reject Jesus as Lord. So that means if someone is rejecting Christ, the god of this world has blinded the eyes of their understanding and altered their right mind to think erroneously. By praying in the Spirit, we begin to change those spiritual influences to give the person the opportunity to get back in their right mind.

Many people contact me and say, "Pastor, pray for me. I'm trying to stop overeating or arguing with my spouse," or, "I need to know God's will for my life." I get all sorts of requests. The first thing I usually try to tell them is, "Pray in the Spirit." Many times I've said, "Go pray in tongues over this for twenty-four hours or thirty-six hours, and then call me back." More often than not they'll call me back and say, "Pastor, I don't need the answer from you. God gave it to me."

I encourage you to set aside some time each day and find a quiet place where you can pray in the Spirit. Of course, you can pray to God in your own mind, and you can accomplish a lot of things that way. But there's something about praying out loud so that your own ears can hear it. Your own brain will hear what you are saying and begin to spiritually discern the Holy Spirit's prayers. It builds a cycle of faith and empowerment.

Build yourself up on your most holy faith by praying in the Holy Spirit. This enables you to develop a dynamic, powerful prayer life that lifts you up on the wings of the Spirit of God and raises you above all the draining worldly discouragers that attempt to rob you of your faith. This all has to do with third-heaven authority. To walk in that level of authority, we must use the tools that God has given us, including tongues.

CHAPTER 11

THE PILLARS OF THIRD-HEAVEN AUTHORITY

*M*ERRIAM-WEBSTER DEFINES THE word *pillar* as "a firm upright support for a superstructure."[1] That's a good definition because there's no doubt that third-heaven authority becomes a spiritual superstructure when built into our lives. Using this analogy, there are three main pillars of truth that must be in place for us to stand firm in third-heaven authority: how to *be* authority, how to *take* authority, and how to *occupy* authority. In this chapter we are going to explore each one, but first I want to lay a firm foundation from the apostle Paul.

In Ephesians 1:15–23, Paul prayed a compelling prayer that plays a major role in what we have been discussing. He starts off saying in verses 15–16, "Therefore I also, after I heard of your faith in the Lord Jesus and your love for all the saints, do not cease to give thanks for you, making mention of you in my prayers." Of all the things Paul expressed gratitude for in the letters he authored, he thanked God most often for the actual believers themselves—those who had accepted the Lord Jesus Christ—and for their Christian lives.

After giving thanks for them, Paul tells the Ephesians his prayer for them: "that the God of our Lord Jesus Christ, the Father of glory, may give to you the spirit of wisdom and revelation in the knowledge of Him" (v. 17). He begins by praying for spiritual things, that God would give them the "*spirit of* wisdom and revelation in the knowledge of Him." In other words, Paul prays that they will have an impartation of power from the spiritual realm. This goes far beyond natural talents, reason, and wisdom. Because we don't have it in our natural state, we desperately need the spirit of revelation, discernment, and spiritual knowledge.

The Holy Spirit Himself, the third person of the Trinity, is the spirit of revelation. And Paul prays that God "may give [this] to you." My prayer for each person reading these pages is the same: that you receive the spirit of wisdom, insight, and revelation concerning these spiritual matters. This spiritual understanding is an unveiling of things that cannot be known in any way other than in your heart. That doesn't mean it's nonintellectual; rather, it's an intimate knowledge that comes out of a relationship with God. This knowledge has to be Spirit-taught. This revelation becomes a part of you because the Spirit of God reveals it, speaks it, imparts it, and breathes upon it.

Paul continues in verses 18–19, "The eyes of your understanding being enlightened"—and, of course, he's speaking of spiritual eyes—"that you may know what is the hope of His calling, what are the riches of the glory of His inheritance in the saints, and what is the exceeding greatness of His power toward us who believe, according to the working of His mighty power." The eyes of our understanding are enlightened so we can comprehend and walk in three things: (1) the hope of His calling; (2) the riches of the glory of His inheritance in the saints; and (3) what is the greatness of His power—the knowledge of everything that belongs to us on the earth because we are in Jesus.

When was His mighty power worked? "When He raised Him from the dead and seated Him at His right hand in the heavenly places" (v. 20). The same power that raised Jesus from the dead and seated Him at the right hand of the Father on high is at work in us. It's part of the spiritual empowerment we receive.

Verse 21 goes on to say He was raised "far above all principality and power and might and dominion, and every name that is named, not only in this age but also in that which is to come." That means He has total power and authority now and forever. And that is our reality too. Remember, Jesus told His disciples, "All authority has been given to Me in heaven and on earth. Go therefore and make disciples of all the nations, baptizing them in the name of the Father and of the Son and of the Holy Spirit" (Matt. 28:18–19).

In the name of Jesus, we have been delegated the right to operate in His authority in both heaven and earth. This authority is from above; He won it by conquest when He died for our sins and was raised for our justification. The Lamb of God who was slain was raised to now be seated at the right hand of the Father in glory. Jesus is not only the second person of the Godhead, but through His resurrection He has earned a supreme place of authority in heaven and on earth. I can't stress enough how critical this is.

In the present, He is the head of the church in heaven, and we're His body on earth. We have His authority, and we go forth on His behalf. The ability comes by the Spirit of God within us. The authority is in who we are, but also by the delegated use of the name of Jesus. His blood purchased that authority and power, and His name releases it. His authority flows from where He's seated in heaven through us to earth. That's why I have repeatedly emphasized that one of the things the Lord showed me when He took me to the third heaven in 2010 is that the flow of authority is from heaven to earth, not from earth up to heaven.

Then Paul says in Ephesians 1:22, "And He put all things under His feet, and gave Him to be head over all things to the church." In the authority He gave to Jesus, God put everything under Jesus' feet and made Him to be head over all things to the church. The word translated "church" in this verse is *ecclesia*. It means a called-out assembly.[2] That word is also used in Matthew 16:18, where Jesus said, "On this rock I will build My church, and the gates of Hades shall not prevail against it." Right after Jesus made that statement, He transferred to the church the authority to bind and loose. As I said previously, I believe He transferred the authority that had been within the Sanhedrin Council in the old covenant to the body of Christ, the ecclesia, under the new covenant. Believers are now the called-out assembly that enforces the laws of God. We, the church, enforce heaven on earth.

The Ephesians 1 passage ends by saying, "And He put all things under His feet, and gave Him to be head over all things to the church, which is His body, the fullness of Him who fills all in all" (vv. 22–23). What Paul is saying here is that Jesus is both in heaven *and* on earth. He is in heaven as the head, meaning He is seated at the right hand of the Father. Jesus is seated there, but His authority extends all the way to the earth because His body extends all the way to the earth. We the body of Christ are all those on the earth who have been born again. All things have been placed under Jesus' feet. And where are the feet located in a body? At the bottom, the part that touches the earth.

Why is this significant? It's important because the passage says, "He put all things under His feet." Again, the feet are part of the body, which is us. That means we have spiritual authority here on the earth to stomp on the enemy. That's why we can bind and loose. That's why we can lead people to Christ and pray for them to be baptized in the Holy Spirit. That's why we can pray for the sick and cast out demons. *Third-heaven authority is all about how we apply our delegated authority.* We train ourselves to see from the perspective of heaven, looking down to earth, rather than looking up from earth and trying to get heaven to move on our behalf. In order to walk out practically what is rightfully ours, we have to know beyond the shadow of doubt that we are with Christ and have His power, which is above our circumstances and the enemy's strongholds on earth.

THREE PILLARS OF SUPPORT

I said this earlier, but it bears repeating: spiritual authority is the delegated *right* to act, while spiritual power is the *ability* to act. If we want the spiritual power, which is the ability to change things—to work the works of God—then we need the authority to do so. No authority equals no results.

In Luke 10:17–19, knowing He was about to leave the earth, Jesus sent the seventy disciples out into the cities in pairs. They went out and returned rejoicing, saying, "Lord, even the demons are subject to us in Your name." To that, Jesus responded: "I saw Satan fall like lightning from heaven. Behold, I give you the authority to trample on serpents and scorpions, and over all the power of the enemy, and nothing shall by any means hurt you."

Jesus gave the disciples authority, the right to walk over the power of the enemy, the ability to act. We are His feet and have that same authority over all the enemy's power, and we also have authority to release God's kingdom into the earth. This brings me to the three pillars I shared with you in the beginning.

1. How to *be* authority. Ephesians 2:4–6 says: "But God, who is rich in mercy, because of His great love with which He loved us, even when we were dead in trespasses, made us alive together with Christ (by grace you have been saved), and raised us up together, and made us sit together in the heavenly places in Christ Jesus." In other words, one of the dynamics of this wonderful life in Jesus Christ is that God has raised us up and caused us to sit together in those heavenly places in Christ Jesus. "To sit" in this passage is simply a slightly different way of saying "to be."

We sit with Him on the throne. Sitting indicates intimacy and rest. Our relationship with Jesus is more about being than doing. Everything, including authority, flows out of that state of being with Him. So the first pillar of support is that we must *be* authority rather than *have* authority. That may sound a little peculiar to you, but authority in Jesus sitting on the throne is not abstract or detached from Him. Jesus is not sitting next to something called authority that He's only allowed to use once in a while. Jesus is the head. He *is* authority. You can't separate the two. And because we are in Him and He in us, we are that authority also. He is the head in heaven, and we are the body on the earth. We have to own this and understand that the authority is within us. When we were born again, this authority became part of our nature. It's part of Jesus' ruling capacity through the church. Why did Jesus transfer the ability to bind and loose in Matthew 16? What was the point? For it to be used! Jesus gave that power to us for a reason.

Because authority is part of our essence now, it's important that we understand how to *be* that authority and let it flow out of us. It's not something we have to pray about and hope God gives to us on occasion. It's already ours. You may just now be finding this out, but it was given to you two thousand years ago. The moment Jesus was raised from the dead and sat on His throne, He released the Holy Spirit into the earth, and the authority was given. We're now learning how to be who we were created to be in Him.

2. How to *take* authority. Paul continues in Ephesians 2:10, "For we are His workmanship, created in Christ Jesus for good works, which God prepared beforehand that we should walk in them." Paul uses the word *walk*, but I'm going to use the word *take*. This is not extrabiblical. Let me explain. After we realize that pillar number one is to *be* the authority, we have to then *take* the authority, or allow it to begin to work in our lives. We rise up and *take* it, which in essence is walking in it. The word *walk* is a verb that communicates action. We actually *take* a walk. So this passage is conveying that we are taking a walk in the things God prepared for us, including authority.

I am in authority; therefore, I take my position. I'm not just hoping the authority will be there. I'm not trying to figure out how to pray the right way or attempting to project my words at the right volume or trying to have enough faith to use this authority. No, I just take it. It's mine. I own it. So I *take* authority over the enemy. I take authority in this situation and allow that authority to work. And I will walk in the works God has prepared beforehand for me and take what is rightfully mine. I often start my prayers by saying, "In the name of Jesus Christ, I rise up in the Spirit and *take* authority over _____," and then I address what I am praying for. It's imperative that we *take* the authority.

3. How to *occupy* authority. By occupy, I mean hold on to it. In Ephesians 6, where he talks about the armor of God, Paul uses the word *stand* three times. Standing is occupying. He says in verse 11, "Put on the whole armor of God, that you may be able to stand against the wiles of the devil"—the schemes, strategies, and deceitful tactics the enemy directs toward us. "For we do not wrestle against flesh and blood, but against principalities, against powers, against the rulers of the darkness of this age, against spiritual hosts of wickedness in the heavenly places. Therefore take up the whole armor of God, that you may be able to withstand in the evil day, and having done all, to stand" (vv. 12–13).

The word translated "stand" in these verses is a military term that denotes not giving up territory. Don't give up ground. Our authority is spiritual territory that the enemy wants to seize from us. So we have to occupy that authority by standing and holding on to it. Standing in the authority that is yours is a matter of actively walking in dominion.

This truth is so exciting because this is where the power is. Demons tremble and are afraid of those who truly understand and have implemented these three pillars. Physical bodies will be healed by their prayers. Evil spirits will flee and their wicked influence will be broken from people's lives. Miracles will happen. So receive the spiritual powers of wisdom and revelation in the knowledge of Him. Then *be* authority, *take* authority, and *occupy* authority in the name of Jesus Christ. These are pillars for operating in third-heaven authority. When the DNA of that word becomes part of you, it's an explosive thing. You rise up as a third-heaven creation operating in third-heaven revelation and functioning in third-heaven authority. You trample on the enemy and place the circumstances of life under your feet!

CHAPTER 12

WARFARE IN THE HEAVENLIES

I N REVELATION 2:20, the apostle John dictated the words from the glorified Jesus in heaven to the church of Thyatira: "I have a few things against you, because you allow that woman Jezebel, who calls herself a prophetess, to teach and seduce My servants to commit sexual immorality and eat things sacrificed to idols."

Jesus knew well that Jezebel was not her real name. She wasn't the actual Jezebel from the Old Testament. He was speaking to the deceiving spirit that was working through this woman who had taken a position of authority in the church. She was influencing Gentile believers to think it was OK to remain socially connected to people and municipal organizations that propagated sexual immorality. Jesus recognized that she called herself a prophetess and had usurped her position by bringing ungodly doctrine into the church. She was attempting to sway the believers from true morality, bring them into a liberal perversion, and derail their walk with the Savior.

The glorified Jesus in heaven called her Jezebel because He recognized the same spirit that was at work all those centuries before. He reached back in history and identified the spirit operating in Jezebel of old as the one now operating through a woman in the church of Thyatira. Because of their familiarity with the ancient Jezebel, Jewish Christ-followers in particular had wisdom for the new Gentile converts who were coming into the church.

137

First Kings 16–21 and 2 Kings 9–11 talk about the historical figure Jezebel and her daughter, Athaliah. Since 2004, the Lord has been revealing to me the influence of that same demonic spirit in America and what He called the "ruling political spirit of Jezebel."

I was aware of Jezebel spirits and how they operated through individuals. I'd seen them at work in congregations, coming against pastors and other church leaders to usurp their authority, just as that spirit was doing in Thyatira. But the Lord began taking my understanding to an even higher level. He started revealing the influence of Jezebel as a ruling political spirit in America.

About ten years later, the Lord gave me a vision. He took me into the spirit, raised me up into the heavenly realms, and allowed me to see over Europe. Looking down from that location, I saw a beast slither its way from the Middle East and settle in Europe, where it worked against the churches for quite some time. Then it dove off the western coast of Europe, swam across the Atlantic Ocean underwater, and then crawled up on the eastern seaboard of the United States.

The Lord spoke to me and said, "That is the beast that empowers Jezebel. It's the spirit I want you to concentrate on, teach about, and actively war against in America. It is the one that is bringing extreme liberalism into American society." Jezebel is a compound name meaning worshipper of Bel (Baal). I began to notice at that time in 2004 that there seemed to be an increase in narcissism and violence among women in the United States. I also observed that the emasculating and belittling of men were also on the rise. Societal norms in our nation at the time were beginning to change. Since then, the Lord has revealed even more to me about the connection between the Jezebel spirit and America's sociopolitical slide to the Far Left. And there is more change coming.

In the Old Testament, Jezebel was the daughter of the king of Tyre and Sidon, Phoenician coastal cities. She was, therefore, a Phoenician princess. She married Ahab, the king of Israel, which was disastrous spiritually because the Phoenicians were idolaters. Their main idols were Baal and Astarte. In addition, Tyre and Sidon were some of the wealthiest and most advanced liberal societies of their day. They were highly developed in the philosophy of social and religious tolerance. However, there was one thing Jezebel was not tolerant of: Judaism and its one God. To Jezebel, serving one God meant there could be only one source of truth, and it was not the god she served. We see that same Jezebel spirit in America today, as it tolerates every religion and perverted lifestyle yet rejects the one true God of the Judeo-Christian faith.

Jezebel was more than willing to use violence and treachery to gain and hold power. The Israelites thought she would bring them social refinement. Israel was a divided kingdom at the time, and the northern kingdom of Israel was landlocked. The Israelites saw their location as an opportunity not only to increase their economic status by trading at the coastline but also to be accepted by the idolatrous people around them.

Israel also entered into a military treaty with Tyre and Sidon. Jezebel used this to bring her idolatry into Israel. She married Ahab, a king with weak spiritual values. He tried to control the prophets and get them to declare what he wanted them to say. He found himself unable to resist

Jezebel's charms, so she became influential in Israel and brought great harm.

Jezebel persecuted the prophets. She had no problem committing murder; she had a man named Naboth killed simply because she wanted his vineyard (1 Kings 21). Jezebel had a daughter named Athaliah, who married Jehoram. He was the prince of Israel's southern kingdom of Judah and eventually became the king. Athaliah followed in her mother's footsteps and led Judah in Baal and Astarte worship. Now the Jezebel spirit was in both kingdoms, controlling the nations from the highest levels. Remember, the Lord called this a ruling political spirit. Jezebel and Athaliah were wicked queens who together had taken over the leadership of the Israelites. God was not happy with Israel and Judah for allowing Jezebel to take control. The same was true for the church of Thyatira in Revelation. God was upset, just as He's upset with believers in America right now for allowing Jezebel to come not only into the church but into the government. We must stand against it with our full authority.

How did God rid Israel and Judah of Jezebel? He devised a plan that took years to play out, but it worked. The Lord also will be victorious over the Jezebel spirit in America today. I'm telling you that in America today, the church of the Lord Jesus Christ can and will defeat the ruling political spirit of Jezebel. We will strip her of her power, and we will take back our nation. We will also rid the body of Christ of her influence.

This is how God rid Israel and Judah of this spirit. He raised up the combined ministries of the prophet, priest, and king. In the old covenant, the Spirit of God did not live within people like He does today. Only after Jesus died for our sins, rose from the dead, and ascended to the right hand of the Father did He send the Holy Spirit to live within us.

We know that in the Old Testament the Spirit of God came upon the ministries of the prophet, the priest, and the king to lead and guide the nation. You may remember the exploits of the mighty prophet Elijah. He had utter contempt for what Jezebel had done to the nation. So the Lord told him to bring judgment against Jezebel. Elijah was not able to do that in his lifetime, so he transferred his authority to his servant, the prophet Elisha. Following God's command to Elijah, Elisha anointed Jehu king of Israel (1 Kings 19:16–21; 2 Kings 9:1–13). Then the combined ministries of Elisha and Jehu, the prophet and the king in Israel, came against Jezebel.

Eventually, Jehu rode into the city where Jezebel's palace was located. Jezebel got all prepped up and ready for the day, and then looked down from her balcony. When he saw her, Jehu called out to the eunuchs who were with the queen on the balcony, "Throw her down," and they answered by heaving Jezebel off the balcony. She was trampled by the horses and then eaten in the streets by dogs. They left nothing but her skull, her feet, and the palms of her hands (2 Kings 9:30–37). It's a gruesome tale, but it shows that God wasn't playing games with idolatry.

Meanwhile, Jezebel's daughter, Athaliah, was spiritually perverting the southern kingdom of Judah. God had a plan for her too. The Lord chose a man named Jehoiada as Judah's high priest to destroy Athaliah. Athaliah had just murdered all her grandchildren to ensure none of them could rise up and contest her power. This is how evil she was. But Jehoiada and his wife had hidden one of the queen's grandchildren, a boy named Jehoash. They kept him in hiding for six years, and then when the timing was right, Jehoiada organized a coronation ceremony.

Athaliah was in the palace when she heard what sounded like a coronation ceremony. When she ran to investigate, she discovered to her surprise that her grandson was still alive and was being crowned king. Athaliah started screaming, "Treason! Treason!" But instead of the army coming to her aid, they followed the priest Jehoiada's order and had her killed. The combined ministries and anointing of prophet Elisha, King Jehu, and the priest Jehoiada brought an end to Jezebel's and Athaliah's idolatry in Israel and Judah. That was in Old Testament times. What about now?

The Bible tells us that Jesus Christ has assumed the combined ministries of the prophet, priest, and king. In Acts 3:22–26, He is called the Prophet of whom Moses foretold. In Hebrews 4:14–16, He is the great High Priest of heaven. In Matthew 25:31–34, He is the coming King of glory. Christ, a name that means Anointed One, has the combined ministries within Himself to impart to the church. We have the authority and power of Christ to stop Jezebel dead in her tracks and drive her out of both our nation and the church.

REMNANT BELIEVERS

God is calling for those remnant believers who will accept the commission, as Elisha took the mantle from Elijah. This remnant will be those who understand who they are in Christ and will rise up in third-heaven authority to stand against that foul, ruling political spirit of Jezebel. It's not just an individual spirit that's operating in a person here and there, but a major demonic spirit that's probably the largest influencer in America.

I know there are many other spirits at work. I understand the spiritual realm, but I am telling you what the Lord Jesus Christ shared with me. He told me to resist that foul, ruling political spirit of Jezebel in third-heaven authority. She has built high places in America. In the Old Testament, high places were located on mountaintops, mounds, or any similar elevated place. The goal was to get as high as they could to worship; this was true not only for those who followed Jehovah but also idolaters.

Oftentimes altars or even small temples would be built on the high places as the people attempted to get closer to God so as to have some kind of spiritual authority over everything down below. In America there are sociopolitical high places in the government, the judiciary, the education sector, the media, entertainment, and even organized religion. Jezebel attempts to overtake all those areas. The apostle Paul wrote about "this present evil age" (Gal. 1:4), referring to the entire mass of human thinking that is devoid of revelation from the Spirit of God. He wrote, "Although they knew God, they did not glorify Him as God, nor were thankful, but became futile in their thoughts, and their foolish hearts were darkened. Professing to be wise, they became fools" (Rom. 1:21–22).

Jezebel not only has these high places but she also has her prophets who espouse and spew her doctrine—liberalism, atheism, agnosticism, secularism, socialism, communism, new ageism, the occult, witchcraft, and everything that is anti-Christ. Saying it with a different emphasis, Jezebel's agenda is anti-Christ's purposes for believers, including you, and anti-Christ's purposes for America and other nations. Everything that is anti-Christ is a doctrine of demons and a false prophecy to our nation. And God wants the high places taken back. He wants the altars of Jezebel torn down. He wants the voices of the prophets of Jezebel to be silenced and their power and influence destroyed.

The ruling political spirit of Jezebel is not gender specific. It will operate through men as much as it will through women. I usually refer to it as "she" only because the demon was hosted by two women in the Bible. It's a liberal spirit—politically, socially, economically, and doctrinally. It teaches tolerance and inclusivity, and it angrily and violently squelches anybody who opposes it. It does not believe in absolute truth. This spirit is also narcissistic. Personal happiness is all that's important, even at the cost of the collective needs of the people. An example is men competing as transgender women in female sports. Who cares about the unfairness to the thousands of biological women as long as the small transgender community is not offended?

Jezebel is also in rebellion against biblical order and lines of authority. It redefines sin as normal and will try to destroy anything that gets in the way of its personal happiness. It's a seductive spirit that uses sex, money, culture, social refinement, and elitism as lures to the flesh of those it wants to captivate.

An idolatrous spirit, it produces slaves to lawlessness and the flesh. It's a manipulative and controlling spirit with the goal of usurping authority and power for itself. It preaches love and unity, but it's a vengeful spirit that will destroy anyone who gets in its way. It is a religious spirit that cloaks itself in the form of godliness but denies the power thereof. It puts on a religious display yet destroys prophetic revelation, truth, and any form of heart-to-heart intimacy with the living God. Moral absolutes and the divine truth found in Christianity are major enemies. It hates God's involvement in society, especially in politics. It sees not only the Bible as a rigid document that must be changed but also the US Constitution. Their rigidity does not allow the Jezebel spirit to accomplish its purposes; therefore, they must be altered.

Such is Jezebel in America today. Her influence has spread far and wide. She has bewitched many with her seductions. She has influenced many in the body of Christ, bringing about a liberal theology where there is no absolute truth. This liberal theology produces an impotence that keeps segments of the church from being able to reproduce itself in true godliness. But I have a message for you, foul spirit of Jezebel, you ruling political spirit.

In the name of Jesus, we rise up with Christ's authority and anointing. In the spirit realm, we go behind the scenes to pronounce judgment upon you and all your works. We tear down all your idols and altars in the high places. We shut the mouths of your prophets who regurgitate your false doctrine in America. We bind your evil work and loose the purposes and powers of God into our nation, in Jesus' mighty name.

I also pray for a spirit of revelation and understanding to come upon you, reader, as you read this book and that the Holy Spirit would reveal to you how the Jezebel spirit has affected your life and your nation. I pray for you in the name of Jesus, that you would have a holy boldness and rise up in third heaven authority to confront her and kick her out of your life, your family, your city, and your nation. As you stand against the Jezebel spirit, I pray that the angels of God will protect and minister to you. I pray also that the Holy Spirit would release a supernatural anointing for youth, health, and strength into your body. I pray for a supernatural anointing for finances to fund everything God has assigned for you to do and enjoy in your life.

Jezebel was driven out of Israel and Judah, and Jezebel will be driven out of the United States of America, in Jesus' name!

A Political Prophetic Encounter

At this point I want to share an important spiritual encounter I had on April 7, 2016. This concerned something that tremendously affected America. At the time, I was leading a midweek intercessory prayer group that had gathered to pray for the United States and Israel. It was a US presidential election year, and we felt the Holy Spirit's unction to intercede for the right person to be elected.

The primaries were still underway, and there were a number of candidates vying for the presidential nomination of each political party. I was using third-heaven authority, praying in the Spirit and seeking God concerning the election. Suddenly I found myself pulled into the spiritual realm. An angel appeared to me on my right side. I heard the angel say, "The dogs of hell have been released against the one with the hand of the Lord on him. Speak against the spirits of false witness, hatred, and murder. Release truth and justice into the atmosphere, and we will break the teeth of the enemy."

While the angel was talking, the face of one of the candidates was superimposed over him so I could see both the candidate and this messenger from God. At that moment the Spirit of the Lord spoke to me saying, "False witness, because they are inventing lies, fabrications, and falsehoods. Hatred, not just anger. It's visceral loathing and contempt, as well as purpose opposition. Murder, because the intent is character assassination and political death. It's destruction of a person's reputation and social standing."

I had been praying for decades for believers to walk in truth and justice. Now the angel was instructing me to speak those two spiritual dynamics into the atmosphere over our nation. Warrior angels stood prepared to combat demonic authority and power. That reminded me of some of King David's bold prayers in Psalms, where he asked for the teeth of the enemy to be broken (Ps. 3:7; 58:6).

When the encounter ended, I was left shaken. I was quiet about it until I returned home and shared the experience with my wife. After hearing my story, she asked if I knew whose face I had seen. I told her I did know, and it was Donald Trump. She then inquired if I was going to share that publicly. I let her know that I probably wouldn't because I needed to be true to the convictions I held at that time. I thank God for my spiritual wife, who encouraged me to talk to the Lord and ask Him what to do.

My conviction for almost forty years had been to keep politics out of the church. I didn't want to use my position to influence people concerning my own political persuasions. I didn't believe it was my job to tell others who to vote for, but to teach them how to vote according to their own convictions and understanding of the Word of

God. Something happened to me that night, though. The encounter grabbed hold of me, shook me, and wouldn't let go. I wrestled with it all night.

The next morning the Lord finally spoke to me, asking if I was afraid to share the encounter. I told Him I wasn't afraid but cautious. I didn't want to do the wrong thing. But mostly I felt it was important to stay true to my convictions. Then He threw me completely off balance by asking me what I would do if He personally changed my convictions.

He said people depend upon me to obey the Spirit without reservation. He revealed that I had to embrace this area with courage so my ministry as a prophet could advance to the next spiritual level. At that point I knew I had to publicly share the full angelic encounter. I shared it the following Sunday, which was livestreamed for anyone to watch.

That morning while I was preparing for the service, the Lord began talking to me again. "The coming revival and spiritual awakening that I've shown you will coincide with the election. This election will shake the structure of the political spirit of Jezebel on the Far Left. There will be a shaking, and Donald Trump is involved in that shaking. Therefore, this is not about politics, but about revival."

The service was one of the most difficult services I had ever preached simply because it was such a stretch for me. As a result, however, the Lord set me free from religious silencing. Ministers must address things that greatly affect a nation.

During the service, I was also honest with the people that the angel did not tell me it was a certainty that Donald Trump would be elected as the next president, although I assumed he would. What the angel told me is that God's hand was upon him and that the dogs of hell were out to destroy him. The angel didn't even tell me I had to vote for him, but I knew it was the wise thing to do. This experience pulled back the veil, exposing activity in the spiritual realm. It provided knowledge, insight, and strategies that allowed me to pray with authority and power. This was third-heaven authority in action.

As I finish writing this chapter, we are in the midst of darkness again. We've seen some victories, such as the overturning of *Roe v. Wade*. Who would have thought? Yet the enemy has raised its head like a wounded snake to strike. It seems the Jezebel spirit can sense what is coming and is putting up a fight. Never before has there been such a celebration and promotion of wickedness in America. We must not let up but come against the spirit of Jezebel in America as never before.

CHAPTER 13

MY OPEN VISION OF THE LION'S ARMY

S INCE I WAS caught up to the third heaven and given my assignment to teach third-heaven authority, I've had a series of additional encounters. This often happens after I have had a major supernatural encounter and a door to the vision realm pertaining to the same subject or theme has been opened. The job of a prophet is more than fore-telling future events; it also includes enlightening people to activities in the spiritual realm. It's to reveal the mind and purpose of God concerning particular issues that are affecting their lives, their nation, and the body of Christ in general.

To be blunt, an antichrist spirit has invaded America. Anyone who is relatively discerning knows this. This antichrist spirit, which was exposed in the last chapter as the ruling political spirit of Jezebel, is liberal, atheistic, agnostic, secular, and spiritually lawless. It seeks to take over, redefine, and control everything that God established in covenant with our Founding Fathers and the spiritual seeds of truth He placed in the founding documents.

After President Trump was in office, the Lord gave me insight and strategies for the warfare itself. This supernatural encounter came in the form of a fully open vision. I call it the "Lion's Army Vision," and in it I saw three major demonic armies that have been launched against America. However, I also saw an army of righteous warriors not only rising up against the advancing demonic hordes but pushing them back. To accomplish this task, God supplied His righteous warriors with three distinct and potent weapons.

One night while I was teaching a class on third-heaven authority, I was suddenly in the middle of an open vision. The Lord took me up into the spiritual realm, and I found myself looking down on a great battlefield from a position of third-heaven authority. From where I was situated on the battlefield, I could see an advancing horde of demonic beings. They were hideous and grotesque and were screaming and shrieking at the top of their voices. Fear, intimidation, pressure, and violence were their weapons and power.

Then I was shaken to my core by the sound of a ferocious lion's roar to my right. When I turned toward the sound, I was amazed to see the Lion of the tribe of Judah as described in the Book of Revelation. He was massive and magnificent and leading an army of righteous warriors clad in full armor. They all had their swords held high as the light of God reflected off them. Strangely, when the Lion roared, it was not only thunderous, but there were words in the roar. Both the roar and the words entered into the backs of the righteous army, an army of born-again, Spirit-filled believers. Interestingly, while watching all this unfold from above, I had the distinct awareness that I was also one of the warriors below.

When the words penetrated the warriors' backs, they came out of their mouths at the same time as the Lion spoke: "You have lost; we have won." And then the Spirit of God lifted the righteous army up and over the heads of the advancing horde of shriekers and screamers. At that, the righteous army began to shout, "You have lost;

we have won." While saying those words, the righteous army was binding, loosing, decreeing, and issuing forth their authority. Also, when the army spoke, the words came out of their mouths as fire, and there were warring angels inside the fire. As the rapid-fire flames and angels hit the demons, their forces became weakened and eventually paralyzed.

Then, similar to the Lion of the tribe of Judah standing tall behind the righteous army, a furious giant beast rose up behind the advancing horde of demons. It shouted the orders, "Scream louder! Yell harder!" knowing that the power was in the screams. But it was too late. The righteous army's pounding was taking its toll. The shriekers and screamers knew they were defeated.

Behind the giant beast to the right and left I could see other demons being held back for future times. Then he turned to his left and said to those future demons, "The shriekers and the screamers have done their job, but they're faltering. You go forward." So they went in among the shriekers and the screamers. Their faces were different, though. They seemed almost normal, except for their sinister smiles. As they moved into position, the beast told them, "Deceive. Bewitch." They readily obeyed, and behind those malevolent smirks was a contempt for those who would dare to be deceived.

The Lion, fully aware of what was happening, firmly countered the beast and his hordes, saying, "Lying unity— the army of lying unity, false unity, ungodly unity, unity of the flesh!" He was speaking of the unity that tries to deceive people into naïvely coming in line with whatever agenda the enemy is putting forth. It's a deceiving unity. The word *unity* was being used to bewitch people into thinking following the enemy's agenda would bring peace. But it was a lie.

Following their leader, the Lion's army began adjusting their formation. The mature and experienced warriors were moved to the front line while those less experienced shifted to the rear positions. Those now in the vanguard positions had experience with lying unity and discerned how to effectively war against it.

Then the Lion of the tribe of Judah spoke again, His thunderous words coming through the righteous warriors: "You have lost; we have won. Fellowship with darkness is prohibited." The righteous army responded to the Lord's words by saying, "Light be!" At that moment, the fire that had come out of their mouths against the shriekers and screamers was changed to light. Revelation, illumination, and truth came forth. And there were warring angels in the light as they had been in the fire. The light came down on the heads of those that were part of lying unity, and they began to weaken.

The beast turned to its right, where the other demons had been waiting in the wings, and commanded, "Punishers and enforcers, join the battle!" They advanced, looking grotesque and hideous, their mouths huge and filled with sharp, jagged teeth. If you've ever seen pictures of deep-water fish with enormous mouths and sharp, pointed teeth, that's the closest picture I can paint of what they looked like. Instinctively I could tell that the size and position of their teeth represented different things. The longer teeth were meant to destroy the leaders of the righteous army and dismantle the opposition from the top down. The power that had been in the voices was now in the bites. The medium-size teeth were to bring intimidation, subjugation, and forced submission. The shorter teeth were to cause strife and compel people to turn against one another.

As the demons snaked forward, however, the righteous army also advanced toward them, unwilling to give up even an inch of holy ground. Up to this point the righteous army's armor had been silver. But suddenly all their weapons and armor transformed to gold, which represents the glory of God. In the Bible, the glory of God is sometimes symbolized by gold, pointing to the fact that it has weight and value. When the armor was infused with the glory of God, the warriors were supercharged with strength and power for the battle. Then I heard the Lion and the warriors say in unison: "You have lost; we have won! The Lion's jaws will crush the jaws of the punishers and the enforcers."

The punishers were filled with bloodlust. They arrogantly enjoyed destruction. All they wanted was to inflict harm and any kind of pain against those that opposed them. The enforcers, however, were more calculated. They knew they needed to subjugate their opposition and place them under false authority. I could tell it was a usurped authority. It was the beast attempting to gain and use authority, but the glory of God had come upon the righteous warriors, so his efforts had little effect. Then the Lord's army said, "You have lost, we have won! The Lion's jaws will crush the jaws of the punishers and the enforcers." But instead of fire and light, this time wind came out of their mouths. It was of the Spirit of God, and just as it was with the fire and light, angels were in the wind. The glory and the wind came together to defeat the beast's army.

The glory and the wind were the presence of God

bringing not only refreshing and empowerment but also the answer. I was seeing an outpouring of the Spirit of God, an outpouring of the Holy Spirit coming to the earth. It was time. I looked up during the battle and saw a clock in the heavens. It was God's clock, the same kind of clock I'll talk about in the next chapter.

The glory and the wind were coming forth, and in my spirit I heard these words: "It's the wind that causes earthquakes. And earthquakes destroy strongholds. It breaks their foundation." I knew the Holy Spirit was saying that in addition to our third-heaven authority, God has given us weapons—fire, light, and wind, all of which are connected with His glory.

A GREAT OUTPOURING

A great outpouring is on the horizon. I can feel it. There is something happening in the air. Revival. Spiritual awakening. We are entering a new Christian era. It's a time when the prophetic movement that is resisting the darkness is learning how to flow with the glory of God. Understand, though, that spiritual awakening cannot be ushered in simply by those who go to church and sit on the sidelines. It's going to come through the righteous warriors, prophetic eagles, and prayer warriors who will stand in faith. It's time, brothers and sisters; it's time.

Dear reader, I pray for you now about this, because at this moment, the anointing that is upon me and this message is being released. May it come into your heart and burn like fire within your bones. May the Holy Spirit cause something to rise up inside you and lead you forth in the power of God and to see His glory cover the face of the earth. God is going to use you. He's going to use your mouth and your authority. He's going to use your witness and testimony. He's going to use not only the things you pray but also the things you say. He's going to use you to lead people to Jesus. You are a critical link in all this. Watch and be open to receive supernatural manifestations of signs and wonders.

The glory of God is manifesting through the body of Christ, His bride. That's you; that's me. It's a great time to be a vessel of the kingdom. Sure, I know there are a lot of negative circumstances in the earth today that affect us all. They are national, political, and cultural. The screamers and shriekers, lying unity, and the punishers and enforcers are trying to impose their will. But in the name of Jesus, God is releasing His anointing, revelation, and power upon His people.

My vision was not imaginary. It was real and biblical. Acts 2:17 clearly says, "And it shall come to pass in the last days, says God, that I will pour out of My Spirit on all flesh; your sons and your daughters shall prophesy, your young men shall see visions, your old men shall dream dreams." As the end draws nearer, this type of activity is going to become more and more common for God's people. Everything I just related to you I saw in the spirit realm just like I was watching a movie in HD. I saw those punishers and the enforcers challenging the authority of God. But they do not get away with it. We do not allow them to succeed. We confront them in the name of Jesus.

Let's rise up right now in prayer.

We speak with the wind of God to come forth against those challenging the authority of God.

We bind their maneuvers now in the name of Jesus. We dislodge their assignment against the body of Christ and against America. We dislodge and break every demonic strategy and dismantle all the communication structure in the name of Jesus. We declare, "You have lost; we have won." Praise God! And the Lion's jaws will break the jaws, teeth, and authority of those demonic armies in the name of Jesus Christ, amen.

God gave me this vision because He wanted me to see that those three demonic entities were behind the attacks. The influence the enemy was trying to exert was directed not only against the United States and many other nations, but against born-again, Spirit-filled people who might let their guard down in the spirit. The vision was a warning for us to not be deceived, but it also revealed a strategy for how to fight the warfare.

One of the other things the Lord showed me concerning the vision was that the shriekers and screamers came in after President Trump was elected to office. They came in to make noise and contest practically everything. They used violence and caused commotion. Their mission was to get attention. Their noise and intimidation tactics were meant to distract people from the real issues. They fabricated, misconstrued, and attacked. They released anger, hatred, and character assassination, and it's still going on today.

The second army, lying unity, came before the 2020 US presidential election. Again, they were attempting to deceive people and cause them to feel like they had to surrender. They had to project unity, but it was a false, fleshly unity. It wasn't wisdom from the Spirit of God. It was the enemy attempting to control people and cause those who were not part of their so-called unity to look like rebellious fools and be mocked as extremists.

The demonic warriors in lying unity reeked of contempt and deceit. "Oh, let's trick them," they must have said. "Let's pull the wool over their eyes, and everything will be fine. We'll bring peace on all sides. We're here to save the day." They are still working their deception today.

The third demonic army was made up of the punishers and enforcers. They came on the heels of lying unity, but just before Biden's January 2021 inauguration. Quickly they set out to chastise and force everybody to come in line with them, or else. They intended to rule the day.

WE HAVE WEAPONS

In some ways, to the undiscerning public these three armies looked legit. They seemed reasonable on the outside, but deep inside they were vile, wicked, contemptuous antichrist spirits. The Lord, on the other hand, gave weapons to the righteous army.

The first weapon against the shriekers and the screamers was the fire in the mouths of the believers. It was spiritual power and authority. In the spiritual realm, it's the ability to bind and cut off the lies of the advancing horde. It was a weapon in their mouths, symbolizing how as we decree, we by faith release authority into the spiritual atmosphere. The second weapon in the mouths of the righteous army was light. This represents spiritual truth and discernment. And the third weapon was wind, which is the outpouring of the Holy Spirit and God's glory coming forth on the face of the earth.

We are the warriors. We have Jesus inside us as well as the power of His blood along with the right to use His name. There is power in our mouths. Jesus said of Himself, "All authority has been given to Me in heaven and on earth" (Matt. 28:18). That means the body of Christ is releasing authority from heaven itself onto the earth. We don't go forward as lambs but as warriors carrying the sword of justice and righteousness. It is our job to stand against that onslaught from the Far Left. And we do so as the righteous army. We say to the shriekers and screamers, "You have lost; we have won." We say to lying unity and its deception, "You have lost; we have won." We say to the punishers and enforcers, "You have lost; we have won!"

I'm convinced the greatest revival that has ever hit planet Earth is now here, and millions of people will be saved. The glory of God is in America, and it is revealing Jesus. We are taking this nation back for Jesus Christ so His plans and purposes for the United States will be brought to full fruition.

THE LANGUAGE OF THE HOLY SPIRIT

In order for us to become more effective in third-heaven authority, it's imperative that we learn how to walk in the Holy Spirit, which includes knowing His languages. The Holy Spirit has languages, one of which is imagery. When God created mankind and the physical universe, He first saw the image in His own heart. He knew what He wanted it to look like. He saw into the future and then released that image through His words. Jesus then took the image in the Father's words and by the Holy Spirit's power created the universe. This includes the earth, plant and animal life, and the human race. Throughout history the Godhead has used that same process to bring salvation and His kingdom on earth. Visions and dreams from the Lord are part of how the Holy Spirit communicates with God's people.

The Holy Spirit does this in a couple of ways. First, He communicates with words and sentences, such as through the Bible or personal revelations He speaks to our hearts. Those words form images. We don't usually see the actual letters or words in our hearts. We see the pictures they represent. The Holy Spirit has the ability to then paint the image on our heart's canvas so we actually see it as a picture of His will and instructions, and what He wants to come to pass. He shows us our future. When we see the Holy Spirit's picture, it becomes a spiritual memory. We remember it, its impact, the emotions we had, and the direction the Lord is taking us. That image becomes our magnetic north. It's our future. By that image, our faith reaches into our future and brings that image into manifestation so it becomes the reality of our lives.

I'm not talking about daydreaming or trying to come up with a picture in our minds by ourselves. We do not make the image. The image makes us. Jesus understood this principle. He taught in parables because He knew that parables, stories about things the people related to, created an image that would help them understand spiritual realities. The supernatural occurrences I'm describing have a purpose. They reveal the nature of God and our divine destinies and assignments. In addition, they uncover the activities happening behind the scenes in the spiritual realm, which are influencing the physical realm around us. They reveal how we can use our authority to impact the spiritual realm and create change in the natural realm.

God has always used supernatural encounters to lead His people. Visions, dreams, angelic encounters, revelation, the presence of God coming upon us and drawing us into the spiritual realm—these are all languages of the Holy Spirit. Of course it's important to submit them to God's Word. The Word of God is the plumb line of all truth. We never interpret the Word of God by a vision; we interpret the vision by the Word of God. At the same time, our understanding of the Word is not perfect. We can conclude, then, that any vision that is truly from the Holy Spirit will not violate the Word of God, but it may violate our understanding of the Word or a particular doctrine. In that case, the Holy Spirit wants us to change our understanding of that scripture.

In Revelation 19:10, John says, "The testimony of Jesus is the spirit of prophecy." I interpret that to mean every revelation, image, vision, dream, or divine encounter we have ultimately reveals Jesus Christ. They point to Him, not us. They also don't point to the problems around us. The revelations may have come out of that environment, but they all point to Jesus and what He is doing in those circumstances. I share the visions God has given me for the sole purpose of lifting Jesus up as Lord and revealing what He is doing to manifest His kingdom on the earth. In these visions there is often an exposing of demonic entities and the strategies they're implementing behind the scenes. God gives us wisdom and His strategies on how to counteract those attacks. He shows us how to pull down those strongholds and gives us weapons to use to bring about change.

My heart is that when you read the visions and revelations in this book, they burn within your heart and impart understanding of the spiritual realm and the power you have in Jesus Christ. I hope you rise up in third-heaven authority and view life from heaven's perspective. As mentioned before, I believe the majority of the prophet's ministry is to reveal the spiritual realm and help people discern spiritual affairs. Credibility is essential to me. To be a credible vessel, there are some practical things that we need to keep in mind.

VETTING THE PROPHETIC

I've invested over forty years of my life in understanding how the prophetic operates. This includes all the ways God's Spirit communicates with us, including the gifts of the Holy Spirit. Here are a few pointers I've learned on how to vet the prophetic process. By vetting, I mean to subject it to careful scrutiny in order to determine whether it is credible.

First, consider how the prophecy affects you. Does it speak to your heart? Does it burn within you? Does it reveal something about Jesus? Does it line up with the Word of God? Being a credible prophetic person requires a close relationship with the Lord based on His Word and His presence. Hang out with Him so much that you recognize His voice and learn His ways. An example is the relationship my wife, CK, and I have. We've been together so long that I know her voice and how she operates. I believe I'd recognize her anywhere and under any circumstances.

It would be difficult for someone to impersonate her without me catching it.

When CK opens up to me, I understand what she's saying because I know her heart. We're one of those couples that can even finish each other's sentences. God wants to have that kind of relationship with you. Jesus said, "My sheep know My voice." (See John 10:27–28.)

Second, all believers have the Holy Spirit and the ability to operate in heaven's communication system, but not all prophetic people are prophets. Ephesians 4 tells us the office of the prophet carries leadership authority and responsibility in the body of Christ. It's different from being used in the prophetic. This is not to minimize prophetic ministry in any way; it's of the utmost importance in believers' lives. My point is that all believers should be hearing from God, but that doesn't make them prophets. It makes them believers.

The same principle applies to teaching. Just because you can teach doesn't mean you're called to the office of teacher. You may be able to counsel and pray with people, but that doesn't mean you're called to the office of pastor. The whole body ought to be teaching, counseling, and praying for people, and the like, but we're not all called into full-time ministry. That's why the Word encourages us to honor our spiritual leaders (1 Thess. 5:12). Jesus affirmed that these leaders were put in our lives to watch over our souls. Remember Miriam, Moses' sister? She thought that since she could hear from God, she didn't need to listen to Moses, her spiritual leader. This attitude angered God, and Miriam experienced leprosy because of it. (See Numbers 12.) We don't want any form of leprosy on our prophetic ministry.

FOUR STEPS IN THE VETTING PROCESS

The process of vetting a prophetic word or supernatural encounter has four main steps: revelation, interpretation, application, and evaluation.

1. Revelation. Jesus said, "When He, the Spirit of truth, has come, He will guide you into all truth; for He will not speak on His own authority, but whatever He hears He will speak; and He will tell you things to come" (John 16:13). If you've seen or heard something in the spirit, think about what the Holy Spirit revealed to you. What did you actually see or hear? How did it come? If you had a dream or vision, did you recognize God's voice or His form? Did it evoke fear or faith? God only leads us by faith, and we are led forth in peace even amid fearful situations.

Consider also whether what you heard or saw helps or hinders your walk with God. Does it reflect the heart of God? Does it point others to Jesus? Be honest with yourself. Don't embellish or be too quick to assume what the prophetic encounter means.

2. Interpretation. Concerning the interpretation, the Scriptures say, "It is the glory of God to conceal a matter, but the glory of kings is to search out a matter" (Prov. 25:2). So we must ask ourselves, "What is God saying?" Sometimes He gives actual words of knowledge about specific people, places, and things. Other times He uses allegories or parables, not literal happenings. If you had a dream about an earthquake, does it mean a literal earthquake is coming or does it symbolize the spiritual shaking of a nation, church, or system? Perhaps it points to a major crack developing in the walls of a stronghold in your life that God wants to bring down.

Think about how the word holds up to Scripture. God will never give you a revelation that violates His Word. He will, however, violate our personal doctrines. The more you know God's Word, the more the Holy Spirit has to work with. If you are not sure what the Word says about the matter, let that drive you into the Bible and to prayer for God to open your understanding of what the Scriptures are saying.

3. Application. When it comes to application, consider what God wants you to do, if anything. The vision or prophecy should provide some wisdom and edification. Sometimes it's a forewarning to let you know that God is in control. "Surely the LORD God does nothing, unless He reveals His secret to His servants the prophets" (Amos 3:7). Let's say you had a vision of yourself driving a car. Does God want you to literally get into a car and drive somewhere? Or does it represent movement and God instructing you to put something into action? Or maybe the vehicle represents your ministry, that it should carry you and not the other way around. As you pray over the word, you receive greater insight.

It's important to be in touch with all your perceptions— the emotions that came with it, the impressions you felt, the colors, and the sounds. All are pieces of the puzzle, and they help make sense of the mystery. God interacts with you through all your senses and emotions because He created them and the sum of them brings about our spiritual understanding. Again, many people miss what God is saying because their doctrine doesn't allow them to hear certain things.

4. Evaluation. The last point is concerning evaluation. As you proceed, take time to periodically revisit the vision or prophetic word. As you do, you will gain further insights. The Holy Spirit leads one step at a time. If you make a mistake, it's OK. Don't be too proud or embarrassed to admit it and make any necessary corrections. Also, evaluate the pattern of the revelation and how it came to you. That's how you learn the way God uses your unique personality and individual gift. No two people hear God exactly the same way. If possible, place yourself under the safe covering of a spiritual leader who understands the prophetic process. And don't get tangled up in legalism. It'll shut you down.

The main point of prophetic revelation is to expose what is happening in the spiritual realm so you can effectively move forward using the weapons and authority God has provided.

CHAPTER 14

TICKTOCK, LOOK AT THE CLOCK

"Tᴜᴄᴋᴛᴏᴄᴋ, ᴛɪᴄᴋᴛᴏᴄᴋ. You won't believe the time on the clock." The words were clear and distinct. There was no mistaking them or their Source. I was praying in the Spirit when they broke through, stopping me in my tracks. Stilling myself, I listened for more, but that was it. The Lord had spoken. "Ticktock, ticktock. You won't believe the time on the clock." As the words replayed in my mind, I instinctively understood that though God was speaking to me, the message wasn't for me. It was meant for Jezebel and Pharisee. He was saying to those spirits, "You won't believe the time on the clock—My clock—and what I have planned." I quickly found a notepad and jotted down the words.

Later that day, while seeking the Lord for more illumination, I was pulled into the spirit realm for an open vision. It's important to point out here that when these encounters take place, they're not a result of my doing. I'm not trying to make them happen. I'm simply seeking the Lord, praying in the Spirit, or worshipping Him.

Once I was in the spirit realm, I looked up and saw a huge clock in the heavens. It was God's clock, representing His timetable for the fulfillment of His plan. The body of Christ must realize that God is not slow concerning His promises. He is above all and controls all, and everything is unfolding in His perfect timing for His purposes.

On the clock's round face were numerous hands. It had

the typical ones—a second hand, a minute hand, and an hour hand—but there were also hands for days, months, years, and centuries. Then, while observing the clock with much wonder and curiosity, I was sucked into it. I went right past the hands into what appeared to be a linear, flat surface. Behind the surface I saw multiple dimensions, and the second hand morphed into what seemed like millions of second hands, each individual hand indicating a different fragment of time that somehow fit together to form a beautiful mosaic of God's perfect plan.

The Lord began to speak again, and as His words came forth, a globe of the earth appeared before me. It was rotating, indicating the passage of time—days and seasons. "There are many threads in the fabric of time," the Lord said. "Remember the words of knowledge I have revealed to you." He was referring to the different visions and words He has given me over the years. All of them have been leading up to this vision. A convergence is happening in the spiritual realm that is impacting the physical. We are living in days of destiny when God's plans and purposes are coming to pass.

When the Lord said, "Remember the words of knowledge I have revealed to you," He was referring to several visions I received: First, in 2010, He took me to the third heaven and gave me the assignment of teaching third-heaven authority. Then, in 2012, He introduced me to Michael the archangel and told me to "be the warrior." (I'll talk more about that in the next chapter.) In 2013, He caught me away and showed me spiritual warfare in the heavens. During that vision, I watched in HD as the angels tore down the strongholds that opposed the coming revival and the purposes and glory of God in America.

(I'll discuss that later in this chapter.) After that, I had the Lion's army vision I shared in the previous chapter.

Each of these visions came clearly to mind when the Lord spoke to me, yet all this remembering took place in a fraction of a second while I was inside the clock watching the spinning earth. Suddenly thousands upon thousands, possibly millions, of human faces began streaming up into the clock. It was then that I heard an angel say with great excitement, "Here they come!"

The faces were of people being born again; they were from every tribe and nation, society, age group, and ethnicity on earth. This was not the great catching away. It wasn't the people themselves but their faces that were flowing heavenward into the clock. Millions were being brought into the kingdom from the four corners of the globe in the greatest revival the planet has ever seen. And I sensed the Lord say: "Continue running with the vision. Stay true to the assignment. Train the eagles. Teach My people about third-heaven authority. Tell them how to soar in the spirit, how to navigate the heavenlies, how to see My form, how to flow with My Spirit, how to be eagles." And He said, "The great harvest of souls is upon us."

A Phenomenon in the Spirit Realm

There's a phenomenon occurring in the spiritual realm—a change, a renewal, a difference that affects how God's glory is manifesting on the earth. In the last chapter we saw in the Lion's army vision the spiritual warfare that's happening and the three demonic armies coming against God's plan. This phenomenon is the flip side. It's showing how Jesus is manifesting His glory and authority in the earth to counteract those three armies and ushering in this great end-time revival. It's not a time for fear and dread but for great rejoicing. Supernatural manifestations, miracles, and angelic activity will fill the lives of believers.

Right now, a spiritual war is underway for the soul of America. The battle is intense, but we aren't losing. God exists outside our time dimension. The fight has already been won, and America is turning back to God. More than that, this warfare is establishing a manifestation of God's glory in America through third-heaven authority. The Lord wants His glory poured out, and His glory has already touched down. In June 2013, Michael the archangel took me into the heavens over America. (This wasn't the first experience I'd had like this, which I'll explain in the next chapter.) He showed me a rainbow cloud of glory that was descending on the nation. That was the first time I had ever seen the glory in the form of a cloud of rainbow colors.

A swirling mass that looked like a rainbow-colored hurricane, the glory cloud did not have the same borders as the traditional rainbow that appears after a rain in the natural realm. Also, in the natural realm, the rainbow has distinct colors. This occurs in the spiritual realm too, except the light emanates from God Himself. We see this spiritual rainbow effect in the visions of Ezekiel and then later John in Revelation.

In the entire first chapter of Ezekiel, this great prophet is trying to describe his vision of the throne of God. He gives us an amazing word picture of the famous winged creatures and the wheel within the wheel. Toward the end of the chapter he says, "And above the firmament over their heads was the likeness of a throne, in appearance like a sapphire stone; on the likeness of the throne was a likeness with the appearance of a man high above it" (v. 26). Ezekiel is talking about the throne of God and a pre-incarnate revelation of Jesus.

The prophet goes on to say: "Also from the appearance of His waist and upward I saw, as it were, the color of amber"—(Heaven has great colors; they are deeper and more brilliant than anything on earth, and because they emanate from God, they have meaning, life, and power.)—"with the appearance of fire all around within it; and from the appearance of His waist and downward I saw, as it were, the appearance of fire with brightness all around" (v. 27). Ezekiel uses the word *appearance* fifteen times in chapter 1, and notice the references to fire. He's talking about the brilliance and glow of what he saw, that it looked like fire. Then he continues by saying it was "like the appearance of a rainbow in a cloud on a rainy day" (v. 28). Ezekiel is trying to describe what he is seeing in a way we can grasp in the natural realm.

The fire, rainbows, light, and colors all around—"this was the appearance of the likeness of the glory of the LORD" (v. 28). But what is the glory of the Lord, really? The quick, easy definition is the manifest presence of God. In reality, however, when you study the Bible, you find the glory is who God is and how who He is affects everything around Him.

When God shows up, something is going to happen. Something changes because His glory makes sure it changes. There is a joyful side of the glory, and there is a judgment side of the glory. The joyful side of the glory is that we bask in His presence. We see that joy side of the glory in all the ways God touches and blesses us—through healing, redemption, victory, salvation, and the outpouring of His Spirit. But there is another aspect of the glory.

Many times, when God moves, the manifestation of His glory brings judgment. God doesn't have to purposely bring judgment. He is not sitting in heaven saying, "OK, I choose to bless you, but I have a problem with this guy." When the glory of God comes, it automatically sets up a situation in which the two-edged sword called the Word of God cuts both ways, "piercing even to the division of soul and spirit, and of joints and marrow," and discerning "the thoughts and intents of the heart" (Heb. 4:12).

When the glory of God manifests in our lives, it judges Satan's ill will toward us. If you can, visualize that awesome swarm of colors described in Ezekiel 1, vivid and inviting yet with lightning flashing in the midst. The contrast represents both God's splendor and His ultimate authority. The Word of God that inspires also convicts. Depending on what's in a person's heart, the glory of God brings either a manifestation of joy or judgment.

There is, however, also an element of the glory of God that involves spiritual warfare, and that's what I see going on right now in the spiritual realm. I see warfare and an army of God, the Lion's army. While caught up in the visions I've shared with you, I've witnessed the warfare. I've seen the army of God as they've gone forth across America. But this warfare is happening over other nations too. The ecclesia is not limited to the United States. This revival is worldwide.

Do you hear the sound of marching feet? Do you hear the sound of angels' movement? Do you hear the trumpet? Can you feel the awesomeness of the living God surrounding you, flowing through you? The Lord showed me that the Lion's army is twofold. The first part is made up of the warrior saints. We would expect that. But the second part of the army is composed of the warrior angels, the hosts of heaven. They are marching, both the saints and the angels. I hear the sound of millions marching. I hear the prayers of the saints.

I hear them taking authority and binding and loosing. I hear the hearts of believers crying out to God, asking Him to move. And God is moving. I hear the sound of warfare in the spirit, but simultaneously I hear the same people rejoicing in victory at the end of the battle. It's because there is no time element in the spirit. I hear the war cries of those in the midst of the battle, with the Word of God upon their lips. I hear the angels rejoicing in the salvations and the breakthroughs happening in the camp.

This twofold army is going forward in rainbow glory, the rainbow of the glory of God that surrounds the throne. Then notice again what happens in Ezekiel 1:28. The prophet says, "Like the appearance of a rainbow in a cloud on a rainy day, so was the appearance of the brightness all around it. This was the appearance of the likeness of the glory of the LORD." The rainbow glory is powerfully bright. In fact, its presence is so powerful, Ezekiel says, "When I saw it, I fell on my face" (v. 28). The glory of God was so strong he couldn't stand. What happened with Ezekiel when he fell on his face is the same kind of thing that happens when the Holy Spirit comes upon us and we fall under the power of the Spirit. We experience God's glory with power. But it doesn't end there.

The rest of verse 28 says, "And I heard a voice of One

speaking." That's the end of chapter 1, but remember, in the original text there were no chapter divisions. Chapter 2 picks up with, "And He said to me, 'Son of man, stand on your feet, and I will speak to you.' Then the Spirit entered me when He spoke to me, and set me on my feet; and I heard Him who spoke to me" (vv. 1–2). Whenever God's power and glory overcome us like this, He wants to speak to us and give us an impartation. Ezekiel 2:3 says, "And He said to me: 'Son of man, I am sending you.'"

God doesn't manifest His glory just to knock you off your feet and allow you to experience His power and peace. His glory always brings an impartation, a sending, and with impartation comes responsibility and authority. When God gives an assignment like He gave Ezekiel, He also imparts the authority we need to walk it out. After Ezekiel fell on his face before God, the Spirit went into him, picked him up, and stood him on his feet. Do you see the symbolism? The glory of God subdues us, gives an impartation, and puts us on our feet. Then He speaks to us, and we run with the vision.

YET AGAIN

In June 2016, I had another encounter in which the archangel Michael again took me over America in the spirit, and once more I saw that swirling mass of rainbow colors moving and flowing. I've seen this manifestation several times in visions of heaven and the throne room of heaven, and it looked just as described in Ezekiel and Revelation. When that swirling mass is over the globe as it was in my visions, it has to do with the glory of God for revival. His glory and authority are allocated through covenant with believers and applied through His government, which operates by His power. Following that encounter, the Lord took me into another vision in which He opened heaven to me and showed me the rainbow of His glory moving. It had already touched down and was moving through the streets of the United States and around the world.

His glory was flowing forward, and when it touched somebody who was open to receive from Him, the person would inhale, and the cloud would enter their lungs, and they would be born again. There were others who already had the rainbow in them, and when they inhaled, the cloud would go in and fill them with the Spirit of God. There were others who were already born again and filled with the Spirit of God, but they had become dry. It had been a while since they'd had a time of refreshing, and when they would inhale, the glory would enter their lungs and refresh them.

As it moved, the glory would hover over certain regions. In those concentrated areas there was an outpouring of glory, and that region would burst with brightness. This brightness was emanating from living rooms, work lunchrooms, congregations, parks, street corners, and even the Internet. It's hard to adequately describe what I saw; all I can say is that I saw this brightness shining everywhere.

In my forty-plus years of ministry, I have watched the glory of God manifest in so many different ways. I've watched the Shekinah, a Hebrew term for the glory of God, come into congregations. In past visions the glory had almost always been a white cloud, but recently it has changed to a rainbow cloud. I asked the Lord, "What does this mean?" His answer was twofold. Number one, He said, "Something's different. We are in a different time, and I am moving differently on the face of the earth and in the body of Christ, and My glory, the rainbow glory, is an issuance of My authority and the authority you have to operate. You are going to take back the earth. You are going to see the greatest revival that has ever happened." Number two, He said, "It is a position of governance. I can't explain that fully right now. Just heed My words."

Third-heaven authority is not just for me. I have an assignment to teach about this authority, but God's desire is for as many believers as possible to learn to walk in it. What's in the third heaven and in the throne room? It's the rainbow cloud of God's glory. Through all these encounters and everything He has taught me over the years, the Lord has been showing me step by step that we are at the beginning of a new Christian era that operates differently.

Within the church age are different eras and multiple seasons. The rotating globe inside heaven's clock indicated this. We are in a new church era that will focus on the authentic remnant believers, not the popular, worldly organization called the church, whom Paul said has "a form of godliness, but [denies] its power" (2 Tim. 3:5, MEV). God always has a remnant. He showed me in the spirit that we are in a time when the remnant is the largest numerically it has ever been. The knowledge of the glory of God has grown to the point that it necessitates a new form of the glory. It's what I'm calling the rainbow glory. We are in a glory revival. A rainbow glory is being poured out that is different from anything we have experienced on earth until this time. And it affects you.

Psalm 24:1–4 encapsulates what we have been talking about. Feel the splendor as you read:

> The earth is the LORD's, and all its fullness, the world and those who dwell therein. For He has founded it upon the seas, and established it upon the waters. Who may ascend into the hill of the LORD? Or who may stand in His holy place? He who has clean hands and a pure heart.

You may have problems. You may have failures and sins, but if you are in Christ, you are cleansed by His blood and His Word. You have a pure heart. You're already qualified to have God's glory in your life.

The psalm continues to describe those who can ascend the hill of the Lord.

> He...who has not lifted up his soul to an idol, nor sworn deceitfully. He shall receive blessing from the LORD, and righteousness from the God of his salvation. This is Jacob, the generation of those who seek Him, who seek Your face. Selah
>
> Lift up your heads, O you gates! And be lifted up, you everlasting doors! And the King of glory shall come in. Who is this King of glory? The LORD strong and mighty, the LORD mighty in battle. [The glory makes you mighty in battle!] Lift up your heads, O you gates! Lift up, you everlasting doors! And the King of glory shall come in. Who is this King of glory? The LORD of hosts, He is the King of glory. Selah
>
> —PSALM 24:4–10

The King of glory includes all that emanates from Him and His glory. This is the rainbow glory. He is strong. He is mighty in battle. He is the Lord of hosts.

One of the reasons He is mighty in battle is the hosts. He wins, but He wins through us. We are His hosts.

AMERICA IS NOT LOST

We are those who have third-heaven authority. We are of the army of God and part of the hosts of heaven on earth! In this statement, I do not want to exclude in any way the angels of God, millions of which are at His bidding and are our partners and fellow warriors. These millions of angels are at our command and authority. They are there to hearken to the Word of God when it comes out of our mouths. I have seen the angels respond when I have bound spirits and released healings.

In the spirit, I see fire and glory over America and around the world. As I said previously, I hear the sound of war, but it's also the sound of victory. I hear the sound of millions of believers marching with the angels of heaven. I also see the rainbow glory of God that has been reserved for such a time as this to be manifest and bring about victory.

America is not lost. There is hope. America is saved because God is in the saving business, not the lost business. He is in the anointing business. Who is the King of glory? "The LORD strong and mighty, the LORD mighty in battle" (Ps. 24:8). He is the Lord of hosts. Jesus is the King of glory. Come, Jesus. Save the people. Save the people and save America.

We win. What does the Lion's roar say, as we saw in

chapter 13? "You have lost; we have won." To the shriekers and screamers we say, "You have lost; we have won." To lying unity we say, "You have lost; we have won." And to the punishers and enforcers we say, "You have lost; we have won!"

CHAPTER 15

ENCOUNTERS WITH AN ARCHANGEL

T HE FIRST TIME I visited the third heaven, I learned the importance of angels engaging in our daily affairs and specifically in spiritual warfare. I had studied angels all my life, had actually seen them on occasion, and understood quite a bit about them. But the day I was taken to the third heaven, Jesus opened the eyes of my heart to a greater understanding of those messengers. He was preparing me for what that meant in my assignment to teach third-heaven authority.

The writer of Hebrews has this to say about angels: "Are not the angels all ministering spirits (servants) sent out in the service [of God for the assistance] of those who are to inherit salvation?" (Heb. 1:14, AMPC). The first thing we see about angels is that they are ministers. It's also important to note that the Greek term translated "angel" means "a messenger from God."[1] God created these beings to carry His message and do His bidding. But the New Testament tells us they are also sent forth to minister for those who will be the heirs of salvation.

That means believers. When we accept Jesus Christ as our Lord and Savior and inherit salvation, we come into the kingdom. The angels of God then are there to work for us, minister to us, and help us in different ways. Let's look at some of those ways.

First, there is a type of angelic being around the throne in heaven that is involved in the worship and praise of

God. They're called living creatures, cherubim, and seraphim by various prophets in the Bible. Revelation 5:11–14 tells us they are joined by other angels in this ministry to God.

The prophet Isaiah records his vision of these angelic beings in Isaiah 6. Ezekiel's description is found in the first chapter of his book. And in Revelation 4:6–8 we read John's account:

> And in the midst of the throne, and around the throne, were four living creatures full of eyes in front and in back. The first living creature was like a lion, the second living creature like a calf, the third living creature had a face like a man, and the fourth living creature was like a flying eagle. The four living creatures, each having six wings, were full of eyes around and within. And they do not rest day or night, saying: "Holy, holy, holy, Lord God Almighty, who was and is and is to come!"

The living creatures eternally see the nature and virtues of God from every direction and in all existing realms, and they reflect those back to Him in worship. They keep the way to God and represent redeemed man before God and before His throne.

Then there are other types of angels that have different assignments related to ministering to and for God's children on earth. In Scripture, we see that angels have the ability to give physical and mental strength. They did that to Jesus in the Garden of Gethsemane (Luke 22:43) and to Elijah when he was on his way to Mount Horeb (1 Kings 19:5–18). We also find that they have the ability to protect and to deliver. Angels stopped Pharaoh's chariots (Exod. 14:19–28) and delivered Peter from prison (Acts 12:7–8).

They also can interpret dreams, which they did for Daniel (Dan. 10–11). They provide knowledge and wisdom, as they did for Mary and Joseph (Matt. 2:13). And they coordinate events, such as Jesus' birth and life and the events of our lives. Angels have the ability to orchestrate and coordinate. The Bible says they were instrumental in giving God's commandments through the Law (Acts 7:53). They have influence in governments, such as we see in Daniel 10. At death, angels carry us to heaven. They will gather the elect during the catching away (Matt. 24:31), and angels will be involved in casting Satan into the abyss (Rev. 20:1–3).

Scripture indicates that there are different classifications or categories of angels that are here for the assistance of believers. The first is warring angels. In both the Old and New Testaments, Michael is described as their leader. These guys are all about spiritual warfare.

The second category is what are called coordinating angels, or messenger angels. Gabriel is their leader. He is the one that appeared to Mary and informed her she was going to become impregnated by the Holy Spirit and give birth to the Messiah.

There are also guardian angels that are assigned to our lives and watch over us, ministering to us and helping facilitate God's plan through us. God's Word doesn't name a leader for them.

Finally, there are praise and worship angels. We know Lucifer was probably their leader before he fell and became Satan. Ezekiel 28:13 seems to compare the prideful king of Tyre to Lucifer:

> You were in Eden, the garden of God; every precious stone was your covering: the sardius, topaz, and diamond, beryl, onyx, and jasper, sapphire, turquoise, and emerald with gold. The workmanship of your timbrels and pipes was prepared for you on the day you were created.

I've personally been aware of the activity of angels in my life and ministry for years. Still, I was extremely surprised when Jesus gave me the assignment to teach people third-heaven authority. It was at that point I began to have the visitations from Michael I've referenced in previous chapters. How do I know it was Michael? Because the Lord introduced him to me during the encounter. My prayer is that the Holy Spirit will reveal to you the activity and ministry of angels around you. Learn to trust that they are messengers of love, grace, and power. They always have your best interests at heart. They are working for you. They are on your side and wish to help you fulfill your destiny.

I want to focus our attention now on one specific angel, the archangel Michael—the war angel. The reason is that warfare is needed to dispel the fog of witchcraft, control and slumber, subjugation and conformity that is over the land today.

A Taboo Subject

I realize the discussion of angels is taboo in a lot of circles. People don't want to hear about them. They don't believe angels can manifest themselves to human beings, speak to them, and direct them. It's a shame that there are ten times as many books on demons as there are on angels. There's a lot of ignorance about angels in general, much less an archangel. I'm not going to try to convince anyone. I'm simply going to share my experience in a way that you'll understand where I'm coming from. You can believe what you want.

It began back in 2012 and continued through 2016. During that period, Michael, the war angel, appeared on multiple occasions. Interestingly, though, the whole time President Trump was in the Oval Office, I didn't see him at all. President Trump was encouraging Christians all around the nation. He was a great supporter of Christianity in America, certainly one of the most supportive presidents in recent history. He also encouraged and accomplished many wonderful things for the state of Israel, including moving the US embassy to Jerusalem. Considering my longtime focus on praying for both nations, I can understand why I didn't see Michael for several years.

He reappeared to me in 2021. We know from Scripture that Michael is called an archangel. He is the prince of both natural Israel and spiritual Israel, and is associated with spiritual warfare. In Daniel 10 he is called "one of the chief princes" (v. 13; see also verse 21). He actually came to help displace a government and bring deliverance to the nation of Israel.

In Daniel 12:1 we discover that he manifests when God's people need to be protected. In Jude 9, Michael the archangel contended with the devil for the right to Moses' body. And then in Revelation 12:7–9, Michael is the one who fought and defeated the dragon. Those scriptures plainly reveal Michael as one of the chief princes, an archangel that is involved in protecting physical and spiritual Israel, and the leader of the war angels.

In 2012, I was praying in my kitchen for some of our ministry partners who were experiencing difficulty in their lives. I was praying against the oppression and persecution that was coming against them as well as the sicknesses and financial difficulties plaguing them. As I was praying in the Spirit, the Holy Spirit pulled me into the spiritual realm. The moment I crossed over, I noticed there were demons advancing toward me. Suddenly, a sword appeared in my right hand. It was given to me by the Spirit of God along with the knowledge that I must use it to war in prayer for the people for whom I had been interceding.

When the first demon reached me, I swung the sword and said, "In the name of Jesus, I curse and I bind." And then instinctively I knew to say, "Cancer." When my sword hit the demon, a surprised look appeared on its face, and it fell to the ground. Then I confronted the next demon. I swung the sword and said, "Poverty." That demon, too, fell. I went through the litany of conditions the people were experiencing doing this. As I was engaged in spiritual warfare, I noticed that a presence appeared behind me. It was not frightening but comforting. I knew he was on my side. The threat was in front of me as the demonic horde drew closer. But behind me was strength. I knew it was an angel strengthening me and helping me. I eventually realized Michael was giving me instruction and direction as I continued the fight.

In the natural, I must have looked like a wild man as I swung around a sword no one could see physically. If any of my neighbors had been looking through the windows at that particular time, they'd have thought I had gone nuts. I was walking around my kitchen, swinging the sword and yelling, fighting an enemy that was invisible to them but real to me. Eventually, when the fighting died down, I just stood there in the spirit. I lowered the sword to my side, letting the blood I could see in the spirit drip off it.

At that moment, the presence from behind me stood beside me on my right hand. I looked up and saw a majestic warrior standing nine to ten feet tall. He had on armor like that worn in Bible days. It was made of leather, not metal, but it did have metal buckles, clasps, and rivets holding it all together. His sword, which he held down at his right side, was dripping blood too. This blood was symbolic because you cannot kill a spirit. They're eternal, so you can only incarcerate them and bind them in chains. When I wielded that sword, I was exercising my spiritual authority against the demons afflicting people's lives.

Then a voice thundered from behind me, rocking the atmosphere. It was a voice I'd heard before. "Mike and Michael, the unbeatable team," the Lord said. That's when I became aware that the angel helping, training, inspiring, and strengthening me in spiritual warfare was named Michael. Instantly I dropped to my knees and became a puddle before the Lord, overwhelmed by His presence and the realization of what was happening. I had been warring with the archangel Michael.

At that time, I didn't know much more about him than what I had read in Scripture. But Michael had showed up for a reason. It was to help me and to train me in spiritual warfare. Then the Lord spoke again: "Mike, you are a warrior. You've always been a warrior, but there have been many things that have come against your life over the years in an attempt to stop that, to rob it from you, to take away your faith and your ability in being effective in warfare." And then His voice boomed, "Be the warrior." Every fiber of my being trembled at the command. I stood up and said, "Yes, Lord, I'll be the warrior." Then the vision ended. That was my introduction to Michael.

I've had encounters in which other angels gave me messages, such as in April of 2016 when an angel told me, "The dogs of hell have been released against the one with the hand of the Lord on him." Then the angel showed me Donald Trump's face and continued, "Pray against false witness, hatred, and murder. Speak truth and justice into the atmosphere." But in 2013, CK and I were on sabbatical in Las Vegas. I was gazing out the window of our room on the twenty-first floor of a high-rise vacation resort, praying in the Spirit and looking out over the city, when I was drawn into the spirit.

I found myself over the continental United States, and an angel met me that I instantly recognized as the one I had seen the year before. It was Michael. We both looked over the continental United States and saw that swirling mass of rainbow colors descending on the nation. I knew about the rainbow cloud from the revelation we discussed in the last chapter, but now in this vision, Michael was showing it to me in a different setting. This rainbow cloud was a massive move of God, an outpouring of the Spirit. A revival was coming to America.

The rainbow glory represented the throne of God and Jesus' covenant relationship with His people, His will, and all that was being done—and the kingdom of darkness didn't like its progression toward America. Angels like flaming meteorites were shooting in diagonally from the side, bombarding strongholds that were trying to contain the rainbow and keep it from touching down in America.

The angel meteorites would hit some of the strongholds and demolish them. I could see from my position below them that demons would come up and try to rebuild those strongholds or create new ones. So they were slowing the descent of the rainbow but not stopping it because they don't have power over God. And as we previously discussed, the rainbow did indeed eventually touch down. You can't stop God's plan. I turned to Michael and said, "You guys are from God. I mean, how come when you destroy a stronghold it doesn't just stay destroyed forever? Why are they rebuilding?"

Michael replied, "Because of the mouths of men. The hearts and mouths of men empower demonic spirits to rebuild those things to oppose the purposes of God. That's why we, the warrior angels, need faith-filled believers to use their mouths and their faith and their authority to empower us to bring about God's purposes."

What a revelation! At the end of that vision, Michael told me that God wanted us to move to Las Vegas, and that's why we're here. That was the second time I encountered the archangel.

THE FOG

Then in November of that same year, 2013, I was in my prayer closet when God gave me another vision that involved Michael. Actually, it was a supernatural encounter. While I was praying, I was instantaneously transported into the spirit realm. As I ascended through the ceiling and over the city of Las Vegas, I noticed Michael was with me. There was a dense fog all around us, and I heard the angel say, "Come up with me again." A sensation of spiritual power accompanied Michael's presence and words. It was both comforting and empowering as I felt the anointing lifting me up in the spirit. We rose in the spirit realm through what appeared to be a thick fog that was covering the United States until we burst into the bright sunlight above it. Think of flying in a jet up through the clouds and finally breaking into the constant sunshine above it. That's what it was like.

Looking down at the fog, Michael said, "Notice that up here, the Lord's brilliance is always shining. It never goes away, but the fog keeps people from seeing it. The presence and glory of God never lifts from them or from the earth, but the fog dulls their senses. It tries to hide God's glory so they think it's gone. They just can't see it, but it's there."

Again, what revelation! The power and kingdom of God are there; people just can't see it. So they think it's gone. That's the effect of the fog. That fog is like witchcraft. It induces drowsiness and fatigue. It diminishes strength. It subjugates and blurs spiritual vision. It suppresses people's spirits and begins to remove their hope.

Michael turned and looked right at me, his eternal eyes piercing. "You need to tell the people that," he said with authority in his voice. In my spirit, I knew the blanket of fog we were seeing over the United States was the spirit of antichrist and the spirit of the world. Michael continued, "This is antichrist's will for America: secularism, hedonism, false religions, witchcraft, deceiving spirits, hopelessness, and the cares of this world. These things dull the spiritual vision of the soul. They induce spiritual fatigue and sleepiness. That's what is setting the nation adrift."

Do you see that? That's what is setting the nation adrift.

Right now in ministry I'm focused on dealing with this fog because the enemy means business, and he is bringing a very real spirit of deception against America. It's even influencing Christians. When God's people agreed with the fog instead of His Word, all they could see was the fog. They were blind to God's glory. Many became spiritually weak as a result. That is the enemy's plan: to weaken and ultimately destroy God's people.

After becoming weak, they became wishy-washy in their faith and simply went along with whatever agenda the antichrist and Jezebel spirits had. Yet from my heavenly perspective one thing was readily apparent: the difference between thick fog and brilliant sunshine is like day and night. The fog was full of darkness. With no visibility, it felt cold, depressing, and death-inducing. Souls and bodies were unable to function the way God created them to operate. People were perishing for lack of knowledge, and it affected them greatly. The darkness that impacted them also influenced the direction of the nation.

On the other hand, the Lord's radiance delights the soul. The warmth and brightness of the light and glory of God that was above all delights the soul. It warms the body and provides great visibility and discernment. It fills people with life and hope. It's liberating and optimistic.

Michael wasn't finished. "Now that Jesus has strategically positioned you in Las Vegas," he said, "you have a unique assignment. He is drawing you into the grid with other prophetic warrior ministries across the nation. Using the tools God has given you, teach His people third-heaven authority." Jesus had already given me that commission, and Michael had spoken it to me the year before in the rainbow vision. He was reaffirming my assignment.

Michael continued, "Here's the simplicity of God's plan: It takes the wind of God's Spirit to blow away the fog, but it requires third-heaven authority to destroy the fog machine."

I knew when he said the wind of God's Spirit he meant a move of the Holy Spirit that captivates men's and women's bodies, souls, and minds and blows out the fog, delivering them from witchcraft, control, and hopelessness and all their effects. The move of the Spirit—refreshing, revival, spiritual awakening—overcomes all that. However, something has to be done about the fog machine, and Michael said third-heaven authority is what's required to destroy it. This is another reason I'm so adamant about teaching this message.

The following year, in 2014, the Lord caught me away in the spirit yet again. This time, I happened to be in Oregon preaching. I was in my room at that particular point, lying on the bed and praying in the Holy Spirit, and boom, He brought me into the spirit realm.

The Lord began talking to me about the power of intercessory prayer, telling me to keep praying and to get the people praying because there's much coming against the United States and Israel. Then He said, "If you will do your job in third-heaven authority and in prayer, then Michael, the war angel, will protect Israel, and he will protect you in the United States."

At that moment, I was allowed to see Michael in the spirit. This time he did not speak to me, and I observed him positioned over Israel, protecting it. As I watched, I heard the Lord say, "He will protect Israel by defeating its enemies, even those that are in political office in the United States." As I already mentioned, while President

Trump was in the White House, I did not see Michael at all. But in 2021 he reappeared to me and said, "The threat against Israel has returned. I want you to pray. The fog that is in America, the machine still needs to be destroyed. I want you to pray. Keep teaching people about third-heaven authority, and we will win in both realms."

My most recent encounter with Michael was in January 2022. The Spirit of the Lord caught me away, and I found myself standing in the throne room behind Jesus and Michael, listening to their conversation. I heard Michael say, "We're almost ready. The angels are prepared." Then the Lord looked down on the earth and remarked, "I have never had so many people who hate Me, and I have never had so many people who love Me. But I will use those who love Me to reach those who hate Me." Then, as if referring to an important upcoming event, He said, "It's getting close. We will release it." Michael then left the throne room.

Aware of my presence, the Lord turned and spoke to me: "This is why you were born. You have taught My people how to walk in third-heaven authority, and you've been faithful in everything I've asked you to do. Job well done." It's as if He wanted me to see that my small part in His infinite plans was important. He continued, "But now we're ready. This is only the beginning, and you will see My true power."

I believe a major spiritual shift occurred the following month. I don't yet know what the full effect of the shift is, but God will unfold His plans according to His timing. I sense that it started in the body of Christ with the Holy Spirit revealing more and more about the believer's authority. I also feel in my spirit that there will be miraculous manifestations of God's power in the natural realm. They will manifest first in people's lives through healings, deliverance from demonic oppression, and other divine interventions. Then we will see them in the socio-political areas that I called Jezebel's high places.

Those have been my experiences. I have absorbed a lot of information and gleaned wisdom. There were principles imparted to me for victorious spiritual warfare. But you don't need an encounter with an angel to walk in third-heaven authority and destroy that antichrist fog machine fed by the ruling political spirit of Jezebel. We must obliterate this fog machine. How do we do that? We do it by continual prayer, understanding that we have authority in the name of Jesus, and yielding ourselves to the Holy Spirit so He influences our minds and spirits.

The Lord gives us spiritual encounters. He lifts us up and takes us into the spirit. He brings us revelation of the Word of God to transform us in every area of our lives. One purpose, though, is so we can pray and speak with authority over our nations. We speak, binding the enemy and loosing the kingdom of God. When Michael told me it was the hearts and mouths of men that empowered the demonic spirits to resist the purposes of God, he wasn't talking about just unbelievers. He also was talking about many believers who are deceived and lending their own personal authority to speak things that are against God's purposes and against revival in the land. But then Michael said Spirit-filled people using their faith and authority actually empower the angels not only to bring about God's purposes but also to destroy strongholds.

When we pray in authority, the angels are there to respond. They hearken to the word of God, not only when it comes out of God's mouth but also when it comes out of our mouths. They hearken to that authority, and they go forth to do God's bidding. Activate the angels by using third-heaven authority. We as the body of Christ, the ecclesia, have the greatest spiritual power. It is up to us to use it and stop the fog. We must not only come against the fog, but we must combat the fog's advancement against those who would give themselves over to it, become fatigued and lulled to sleep, and then allow witchcraft to enter their lives and rob their third-heaven authority. We keep praying. The rainbow revival from the throne of God is here, and it is moving across this land.

Instead of giving in to the fog of fear and disillusionment, let's move with the glory and allow the angels to follow after our faith and authority in destroying the fog machine. Let's tear down every one of Jezebel's high places—in government, the media, the entertainment industry, the judicial system, and the educational structure—and the influence she has over them.

Jezebel has set up her high places, or her altars. She has prophets who spew her doctrine. And so we must continue to speak against those, bind them, and release the power and glory of God. Releasing power and glory are just as important. We are not just binding what the devil is doing; we are releasing what God is doing.

As I close this chapter, I invite you to join me in prayer for your nation. My encounters were glimpses into the spiritual realm over the United States, where I live. However, these concepts of warring for a nation are true and effective anywhere in the world.

God, save this nation! We pray for a move of the Holy Spirit, the wind to blow away the fog so people can see that Jesus is the way, the truth, and the life, and so revival and spiritual awakening can flow unhindered. In Jesus' name we speak deliverance, we decree salvation, and we use our authority against the fog machine. Jezebel, you are cut off. Antichrist, you are cut off. High places, you are torn down. In Jesus' name, angels be released to accomplish it.

I also want to pray for you, reader. I pray for a revelation upon everyone reading this book. I pray for revelation and anointing to flow across the pages and into your heart. I bless you and decree that you are well able to take your own personal land: your life, your family, your job, and your community. I give You the glory for it, Father. In Jesus' name, amen!

CHAPTER 16

THESE SPIRITUAL BLESSINGS ARE YOURS

B EFORE WE DIVE into this final chapter, let's take a brief overview. Third-heaven authority encompasses knowing who we are in Christ and the authority that has been delegated to us. But more than that, it enables us to operate from a heaven-to-earth perspective rather than from earth to heaven. The difference is life-altering. When operating from our natural, earth-to-heaven perspective, we are attempting to deal with life's situations, both physical and spiritual, from a linear position. This causes us to bend or give way to the pressures and forces coming upon us. Jesus, however, has not only given us a *position* of authority; He has given us a *location* from which to exercise that authority that allows us to operate from heaven's perspective.

In this book we've already covered a good bit of information about Paul's letter to the Ephesians. That's because Ephesians is what I call the third-heaven epistle. Colossians and Philippians deal with some of the same concepts, but there's a special dynamic about Ephesians that became clear to me through my heavenly encounters. When I was in the third heaven the first time in 2010, I began to realize that many of the concepts I understood from my position in heaven looking down matched much of what Paul had written after his heavenly encounters.

We saw earlier that the first heaven consists of the created universe—the earth, moon, stars, and galaxies. The second heaven is the spiritual realm that surrounds the first heaven. This is where the activity of angels, demons, human spirits, and the Holy Spirit takes place. We were created to operate in both realms simultaneously. We have a physical body operating in the first-heaven realm and a spiritual body operating in the second-heaven realm. Then there is the third heaven, which is the dwelling place of God. This is what we typically refer to as heaven, the place we go after death to be with the Lord. What most believers fail to realize, though, is that we also have the ability to operate in third-heaven realities while on earth. The third heaven is not just somewhere we go when we pass on into eternity. It's for the here and now.

Ephesians describes those concepts so well, and we've covered many of them in this book. Yet there are more nuggets to unearth. After identifying himself as an apostle and making it clear who his audience is, Paul greets his readers with, "Grace to you and peace from God our Father and the Lord Jesus Christ" (Eph. 1:2). This may seem irrelevant, but it's significant. Paul often started his epistles with the words, "Grace and peace to you." "Grace," *charis* in the Greek, refers to the unmerited favor and empowering presence of God. This grace enables us to be who God created us to be and to do what He has called us to do. All of it, however, is because Jesus made a way for us through His sacrifice. The word translated "peace" in Ephesians 1:2 is the Greek term *eirēnē*, which refers to an undisturbed quiet. This comes when we operate from the spiritual realm and aren't controlled by our natural circumstances.

Paul moves on in verse 3 to say, "Blessed be the God and Father of our Lord Jesus Christ, who has blessed us with every spiritual blessing in the heavenly places in Christ." As I mentioned before, there are a total of twenty-five "in Christ" scriptures in Ephesians: thirteen occur in chapter 1, nine in chapter 2, and three in chapter 3. All of them point to what Jesus has done for us within Himself and to what God has created us to be within Jesus. Everything is made possible through Jesus. He is our Savior (John 14:6), the firstborn from the dead (Col. 1:18), and the firstborn of many children who are new creations in Him (Rom. 8:29). Because of Jesus, we are third-heaven creations operating in third-heaven realities and functioning in third-heaven authority. We walk in the spirit and natural realms simultaneously.

When Paul writes that God "has blessed us with every spiritual blessing in the heavenly places in Christ," that means all the blessings of God are accessible to us and are spiritual in nature. Our divine destiny is not dependent upon the family, nation, or culture we were born into. It's based upon the culture of heaven itself. All the blessings of God have been equally given to everyone who accepts Jesus Christ as their Lord and Savior. We all have access to "every spiritual blessing in the heavenly places in Christ." You don't have to earn it. It's not something you have to work up. Brownie points are not amassed so you can get more. It's all there for you. Everything. As a born-again child, you are automatically qualified.

So in Ephesians 1:3, when Paul says God has "blessed us with every spiritual blessing," he's saying we have been blessed with themes and strategies that are of a spiritual nature. There is a physical essence where God has blessed us. Healings, answered prayer, and natural gifts and talents are some of the blessings of the physical essence, but that's not what Paul is talking about here. He's refer-ring to spiritual promises, revelation, empowerment, and authority. God uses the spiritual blessings to manifest the physical blessings. The first three chapters of Ephesians are purely about our being, our creation, and who we are in Christ. Chapters 4 through 6 are about how we walk out that identity in the physical realm. These spiritual blessings are things Jesus has already given to us as God's children.

One of the reasons it's critical that we understand this is that when we finally grasp what has been given to us, we realize we can't supply these spiritual blessings. Only Jesus can. Our actions do have a bearing on whether we receive and walk in what is ours, but they don't produce those blessings. Jesus qualified us to receive them through His sacrifice on the cross.

Anything Scripture says Jesus has given to you is part of your inheritance in Him, and it's one of the spiritual bless-ings in the spiritual realm. You are qualified to receive it solely because of Christ's shed blood, not because of anything you are doing in the natural realm. You can't earn it. The moment we receive Jesus as Lord and Savior, we inherit all the spiritual blessings. Life then becomes about learning what we have received and allowing those empowerments to start operating through us. This is a lifelong process.

But notice Ephesians 1:3 also says we have been blessed "with every spiritual blessing in the heavenly places in Christ." The word *places* is italicized in many translations. Why? Windell Gann's commentary on the Bible says, "The word 'places' is in italics, showing that the word as such is not in the Greek text, and is supplied by the translators in an attempt to make plain to the English reader, the thought in the Greek text."[1] In this verse, the word translated "heavenly" (*epouranios*) is an adjective that stands alone, meaning it doesn't modify a noun, and as such it literally means "in the heavenlies," according to Gann's commentary. It refers to a realm "in or above heaven, existing in heaven, the heavenly regions; i.e., the abode of God and angels."[2] We've been blessed with every spiritual blessing in the realm "above heaven" in "the abode of God and angels"—the third heaven.

FUNCTIONING EFFECTIVELY

All this relates to our functioning effectively in third-heaven authority. We have authorization to operate in all three levels of the heavens. That's why on my first visit to the third heaven, the Lord turned me around and had me look through a portal all the way down to earth to the exact spot where I was praying. From the third heaven I was looking through the second heaven and observing the first heaven, the natural realm. My view encompassed all three heavens. Then the Lord told me, "Launch your warfare from here." This transformed the way I perceived and waged spiritual warfare. We have been blessed with every spiritual blessing in the heavenlies, all three realms, in Christ Jesus.

Paul lists some of those spiritual blessings in the first part of Ephesians 1, and then in verses 15–17 he writes:

> Therefore I also, after I heard of your faith in the Lord Jesus and your love for all the saints, do not cease to give thanks for you, making mention of you in my prayers: that the God of our Lord Jesus

Christ, the Father of glory, may give to you the spirit
of wisdom and revelation in the knowledge of Him.

The use of "spirit of" in this passage signifies the spiritual manner in which these blessings play out. Part of that
is a spiritual power, a spiritual gift of wisdom and revelation in the knowledge of the Lord Jesus Christ. Wisdom
and revelation about these truths are spiritual endow-
ments or powers God has given to us in the heavenly
places. That's one of the reasons we can operate in third-
heaven authority from here on earth. It all comes through
our knowledge of Him.

Ephesians 1 goes on to say in verses 18–20:

> ...the eyes of your understanding being enlightened;
> that you may know what is the hope of His calling,
> what are the riches of the glory of His inheritance
> in the saints, and what is the exceeding greatness
> of His power toward us who believe, according to
> the working of His mighty power which He worked
> in Christ when He raised Him from the dead and
> seated Him at His right hand in the heavenly places.

Paul is now describing the kind of power that has
worked to get us saved and is continuously working
through us in our lives here on earth. It is the same power
that raised Jesus from the dead. That is great news, but
how many actually take full advantage of that power?
Again, walking in these realities is a lifelong learning process, but we should be pursuing a greater understanding
of these truths.

Notice in the previous passage that "the exceeding
greatness of His power toward us who believe" is manifest

through the resurrection of Jesus and actually incorpo-
rates the powers of God. It took God's incalculable power
from heaven being poured into Jesus for Him, while in
human flesh, to endure inconceivable torture, die for our
sins, and then be raised from the dead. That same power
is at work in us. It raised us from the dead spiritually,
dwells inside us, will transform us in the resurrection, and
is available 24/7. In verse 19 are four Greek terms that have
the same general meaning of power.

The word *power* in the phrase "exceeding greatness of
His power" is the Greek term *dunamis*. It's talking about
inherent power. In the phrase "according to the working,"
the word translated "working" is *energeia*, which is
power being exercised as energy. The inherent power and
strength had to be released.[3]

In the phrase "of His mighty power," the Greek word
translated "mighty" is *ischys*, which refers to endowed
power.[4] And then the word translated "power" in that
phrase is the Greek term *kratos*, which is dominion, or
ruling power and strength.[5] All the inherent power that
made God who He is was released as energy into Jesus
as the rulership of God took over and raised Him from
the dead and endowed Him with His position in heaven.
That's the kind of power that is at work inside us. Power in
this sense is the *ability* to act, while authority is the *right*
to act. Third-heaven authority is the ability and the right
to function in the power that has been placed within us.

Continuing in Ephesians 1, Paul tells us in verses 20–21
that God worked this power "in Christ when He raised
Him from the dead and seated Him at His right hand in
the heavenly places, far above all principality and power
and might and dominion, and every name that is named,

not only in this age but also in that which is to come." After Jesus rose from the dead, He was seated "far above," not only in a ruling position but in an actual location far above all principality and power, might and dominion, and every name that is named.

The final two verses of Ephesians 1 add, "And He put all things under His feet, and gave Him to be head over all things to the church, which is His body, the fullness of Him who fills all in all" (vv. 22–23). That means God put everything in the known universe under Jesus' feet, "and gave him to be head over all things to the church"—the ecclesia—"which is His body, the fullness of Him who fills all in all."

Jesus Himself said, "All authority has been given to Me in heaven and on earth" (Matt. 28:18). As I stated previously, the power flow is from heaven to earth. The authority is from heaven to earth, and "all things" have been placed under Jesus' feet. Where are His feet? They're in His body. The body is the ecclesia, the church on earth. That means "all things" have been placed under us. Jesus is administrating that authority from heaven through His body on earth.

Is this not what Jesus affirmed in Matthew 16? He told Peter in verses 18–19:

> And I also say to you that you are Peter, and on this rock I will build My church, and the gates of Hades shall not prevail against it. And I will give you the keys of the kingdom of heaven, and whatever you bind on earth will be bound in heaven, and whatever you loose on earth will be loosed in heaven.

As we discussed in previous chapters, the word *bind* means to declare unlawful or to lock up; to forbid. The phrase "will be bound in heaven" can also be translated "will have [already] been bound in heaven" (v. 19, AMP), because the power to do this is in Christ and what He has done on the cross. "Whatever you loose on earth"— meaning whatever you unlock, declare lawful, or permit— "will be loosed in heaven," or again as the Amplified Bible puts it, "will have [already] been loosed in heaven." That means we are the adjudicators. The Greek word *ecclesia* is a "called-out assembly." In Greece during Jesus' day, an ecclesia was a convened assembly of citizens that conducted civil affairs, including legislating and adjudicating.[6] We are the body of Christ that is called out to adjudicate the laws of the kingdom of heaven. Whatever has been forbidden or allowed in heaven we have the authority to forbid or allow here on earth and in the second heaven. That's the reason "all things" are placed under our feet.

✳✳✳

Moving on to Ephesians 2, Paul says in verses 1–3: "And you He made alive, who were dead in trespasses and sins, in which you once walked according to the course of this world, according to the prince of the power of the air [talking about Satan and demonic powers], the spirit who now works in the sons of disobedience, among whom also we all once conducted ourselves in the lust of the flesh [that was pre-salvation], fulfilling the desires of the flesh and of the mind, and were by nature children of wrath, just as the others."

Paul goes on to say in verses 4–10:

But God, who is rich in mercy, because of His great love with which He loved us, even when we were dead in trespasses [because we accepted Jesus], made us alive together with Christ (by grace you have been saved), and raised us up together, and made us sit together in the heavenly places [the heavenlies] in Christ Jesus, that in the ages to come He might show the exceeding riches of His grace in His kindness toward us in Christ Jesus. For by grace you have been saved through faith, and that not of yourselves; it is the gift of God, not of works, lest anyone should boast. For we are His workmanship, created in Christ Jesus for good works, which God prepared beforehand that we should walk in them.

Not only did God raise Jesus from the dead and place Him far above all principality and power and might and dominion, but He raised us up to sit with Him above all. I don't know about you, but that excites me!

Paul ends Ephesians 2 by talking about us becoming one. There is no more Jew and Gentile. There's no distinction other than the new creation in Christ Jesus. We are one new person by the Spirit of God (vv. 11–22).

Paul goes on to say in Ephesians 3, "To me, who am less than the least of all the saints, this grace was given, that I should preach among the Gentiles the unsearchable riches of Christ" (v. 8). The wealth of who we are in Christ may seem unsearchable and unfathomable, yet the Holy Spirit inside us is our teacher, and He reveals these riches to us as we listen to His voice and His illumination of the Word of God. Everything we need has been placed in our spirits. When the Holy Spirit comes to live within us, He brings all God's knowledge with Him because He is God.

The whole counsel and logic of God (*logos*) is in there, and it becomes the Holy Spirit's job to teach us precept upon precept, line upon line each revealed word (*rhema*). That's how revelation knowledge comes to us.

Paul adds in Ephesians 3:9, "And to make all see what is the fellowship of the mystery." The word translated "mystery" here is the same word Paul used in Ephesians 1; it is the Greek term *mystērion* and refers to secret things that are being revealed. This verse is not talking about secret things we can never know. It is speaking of things of the spiritual realm—the secrets of the kingdom, salvation, and the heavenlies—that are being released to us. In secret societies, you have to be a member to be privy to the secrets and receive certain benefits. Likewise, once we come into the kingdom, God starts revealing His mysteries to us. But notice what these mysteries are: "which from the beginning of the ages has been hidden in God who created all things through Jesus Christ; to the intent that now the manifold wisdom of God might be made known by the church to the principalities and powers in the heavenly places [the heavenlies]" (vv. 9–10).

We who are new creations in Christ are releasing through the heavenlies to all its entities the wisdom of God and His divine intent. I realize that is hard to wrap our minds around, but it's what the scripture says: "that now the manifold wisdom of God might be made known by the church to the principalities and powers in the heavenly places [the heavenlies]." All the mysteries that have been given to us are being released through the church.

When Paul says "to the principalities and powers in the heavenly places," in this context he's primarily talking about the angelic hosts who are witnessing God's plan for the ages unfold. The angels are watching God's power manifest, not only in the church age through the body of Christ, but also in particular individuals when His plans and purposes for them are released. The angels then have the responsibility to help those things come to pass. That's one of the aspects of third-heaven authority that is so dynamic. Jesus is better able to use us to release those mysteries into the earth. At that point, the angels hearken unto the Word of God, even as it's coming out of us in faith through our words and actions.

Paul continues, "...that you, being rooted and grounded in love, may be able to comprehend with all the saints what is the width and length and depth and height." Paul then pauses before saying, "...to know the love of Christ which passes knowledge; that you may be filled with all the fullness of God" (vv. 17–19). What's critical here is to comprehend that all of this, including third-heaven authority, is enveloped in the love of God. Without the love of God, we are nothing more than clanging cymbals (1 Cor. 13:1).

The love of God is operating through us. But how can you know something that "passes knowledge," or is unknowable? "[That you may really come] to know [practically, through experience for yourselves] the love of Christ, which far surpasses mere knowledge [without experience]; that you may be filled [through all your being] unto all the fullness of God [may have the richest measure of the divine Presence, and become a body wholly filled and flooded with God Himself]!" (Eph. 3:19, AMPC). We experience these things as we walk them out in God. The Holy Spirit illuminates our path as we allow Him to guide. As Jesus promised, "When He, the Spirit of truth, has come, He will guide you into all truth" (John 16:13).

YOUR ARMOR IS ALREADY ON; JUST ACTIVATE IT

To stay on our theme, we're going to skip past chapters 4 and 5 of Ephesians and probe chapter 6, where Paul is starting to bring his letter to a close. In verse 10 he says, "Finally, my brethren, be strong in the Lord and in the power of His might." Our empowerment and strength to walk in these things comes from the Lord, not ourselves. It's not natural strength, willpower, or determination. It's not strength of the flesh. It is not strength of the intellect. It's strength from the Lord. Unconditional and persistent, it never changes and is always enough. But we have to activate His power in our lives and against our enemy. How? Follow the thread here until the conclusion. Paul ties it all together.

In verse 11 he tells us, "Put on the whole armor of God, that you may be able to stand against the wiles of the devil." Third-heaven authority is not only about loosing, but also about binding. Loosing involves establishing the kingdom of heaven on earth and manifesting the will of God here in this life. The binding aspect, however, is the blocking of those things that are anti-Christ and opposed to what God is doing. Those are the things of the world and of the enemy. That's why Paul says we must be equipped to stand against the wiles of the devil.

"We do not wrestle against flesh and blood" (Eph. 6:12). The warfare we are engaged in has nothing to do with anything of the natural realm, though our prayers impact the natural realm. Whether somebody or something is opposing you—a family member, a friend, something sociological in the nation—those people and things are not what we are warring against, even if they are problematic. There may be laws and conditions that are totally against God's will for our lives, but turning things around starts in this spiritual realm, not with our flesh and our own power. We do not wrestle against flesh and blood.

Consider where we wrestle in this third-heaven authority. We wrestle "against principalities, against powers, against the rulers of the darkness of this age, against spiritual hosts of wickedness in the *heavenly places*" (Eph. 6:12, emphasis added). Here, Paul is talking about those entities (demonic spirits) that work for the devil, fulfilling his wiles (his deceptions and evil schemes). Just as there are different levels of angels, there are different levels of demonic spirits. There are archangels, warrior angels, worship angels, messenger angels, guardian angels, and more. Demonic spirits are similar. Principalities are the leaders, then come powers. After that are the "rulers of the darkness of this age," referring to this system, order, and realm around us. And then there are "spiritual hosts of wickedness in the heavenly places [heavenlies]." We are operating against these wicked spirits in the heavenlies. The heavenlies is not only where all our spiritual blessings are located but also the place from which we wield our third-heaven authority. It's a vantage point high above all principalities and powers. It's where we access God's power flow.

With this understanding, we therefore are to "take up the whole armor of God" (Eph. 6:13). Earlier I shared that in my vision when I was in the throne room of heaven looking down to earth, the Lord said, "Launch your warfare from here." When He said that, the first thing that came to my mind was, "I thought I'm supposed to have armor on when I do spiritual warfare, but I'm up here in heaven. Why do I need armor?" The Lord cleared that up very quickly and showed me that the armor is part of us as new creations in Christ. It's within us. In other words, the armor of God is not something we have to pick up and try to put on. It's not external or separate from us; it is something that has already been given to us. We "put it on" by accepting the understanding and revelation of that part of our new creation and using it against the trickery of the enemy.

Paul goes on to instruct, "Stand therefore, having girded your waist with truth" (Eph. 6:14). In other words, we must receive the understanding and revelation that in God lies all truth. Even if physical facts are opposed to it, God's truth overrides those physical facts. The truth of God's Word and who we are in Him is what protects us. It becomes the belt around our waist that girds up all the apparel, and we hang our swords on it.

Then he says, "...having put on the breastplate of righteousness" (Eph. 6:14). Again, Paul is talking about understanding that we are the righteousness of God in Christ and have been made right with Him. It's recognizing that we are holy because the Spirit of holiness has come into us. Embracing all these truths counteracts the enemy's attack. They neutralize fear, condemnation, and the other tactics the devil uses to hinder us from releasing and walking in the blessings God has given us.

Paul then says to "shod your feet with the preparation of the gospel of peace" (Eph. 6:15). This is understanding the gospel, the good news, and the reality that we accept

Christ and are saved by faith. Our footing in the Lord is stable and will not slip from under us. Nothing the enemy tells us or tries to throw against us can remove that. We are at peace with God because He promises us peace. We have the authority of His Word. And the power of God is going to back us up. Remember, we saw in Ephesians 1 that all these things are activated through the knowledge of Jesus Christ. You know the old saying "Knowledge is power." Well, in this case it is certainly true! The power of God comes through the knowledge of God's truths.

"Above all," Paul adds, "taking the shield of faith with which you will be able to quench all the fiery darts of the wicked one" (Eph. 6:16). The shield of faith can deflect everything the enemy throws against us. Because by faith we are seated with Christ in the third heaven, high above the demons' activity, our spiritual authority can be released and deflect the enemy's attacks.

Ephesians 6 then tells us to "take the helmet of salvation" (v. 17), referring to the understanding that we are actually new creations in Christ. When you are saved, nothing can take that away from you. We also have "the sword of the Spirit, which is the word of God" (Eph. 6:17). You have at your disposal the Word of God, which is a double-edged sword. When you speak God's Word and release it in faith, the Word cuts the enemy to shreds.

Paul goes on to instruct us to pray "always with all prayer and supplication in the Spirit" (Eph. 6:18). One of the main ways we release heaven's will is through prayer. We successfully resist the devil by speaking against his onslaughts in prayer. Let me tell you a story. The Lord took me to the third heaven one time and showed me what I call a revelation room. I'm sharing this because the armor and power of God released in our lives are all about revelation and understanding our identity in Him.

In the vision, the Lord showed me a large circular building. I was standing in front of it, with Jesus standing on my left side. There was a porch with steps going up to the front door. We walked up these stairs, and Jesus opened the door.

Immediately inside was a foyer-like entry. The Lord stopped there and said, "This is the salvation door and room. This is how you get into the revelation building. Revelation is not just knowledge, a concept, an idea. Revelation is an area."

Trying to explain these things in physical terms is somewhat difficult, but the concept is this: There is an area you enter where the Holy Spirit reveals truth and quickens it in your spirit so you ultimately understand. The Lord said, "People, when they accept Me, get saved and they occupy the room." It's not that you simply believe in salvation. You move in and occupy the revelation-of-salvation room. You take ownership. You have dominion, and authority is released.

Then in the vision, Jesus went to the other end of the room and opened a door to a hallway. The hall went straight through this large building. There were circular halls that conformed to the round shape of the building, which put me in the mind of the Pentagon in Washington, DC. The Lord pointed down one of the halls to another room and said, "That's the baptism in the Holy Spirit room." He pointed to another one and said, "That's the healing room."

The Lord began to point out love, grace, and other names for all these different rooms, which are all revelations. And then He said, "You have to go into those rooms, take ownership, take dominion, and use authority, and they become yours. That's how revelation works. That is how the armor of God works."

After we are saved by grace, not works, we occupy by living in the awareness of the presence of God by "praying always with all prayer and supplication in the Spirit" (Eph. 6:18).

✳✳✳

The reason I've gone through these insights in Paul's letter to the Ephesians is to enlighten our thinking about spiritual blessings in the heavenlies. But it's also so we all will understand how to use our third-heaven authority to release spiritual blessings and wage spiritual warfare. This impacts our natural lives and circles of influence on the earth. We are called to release the kingdom of heaven in the culture we live in. That's the way the body of Christ was intended to function. Jesus created us this way.

Another way to say it is that God created us in Christ Jesus for good works, for the manifestation of His kingdom through us. The more we learn about operating in these spiritual realities, the greater impact we will have, the greater the joy and sense of satisfaction we will have, and the more Jesus will be able to reveal Himself through us.

GO OUT WITH AUTHORITY AND IMPACT THE WORLD

A S OUR JOURNEY comes to an end, my prayer is that the Holy Spirit will crystallize these truths in your heart so they become yours. We are entering a time of unparalleled chaos, political upheaval, and depravity. We see Romans 1:28 playing out right before our eyes: "And even as they did not like to retain God in their knowledge, God gave them over to a debased mind, to do those things which are not fitting."

We are living in days where debased thinking and insanity reign. The culture has kicked God out —and lost its common sense in the process. Arrogance and evil are celebrated as moral while true righteousness and sound judgment are treated as hateful and evil. The enemy seems to be advancing and taking territory in the minds and souls of this generation.

Never before in history has it been more critical for God's people to walk in third heaven authority. We must shift our perspectives from a linear, earth-to-heaven view to a heaven-to-earth view. When we do, everything changes. Our spiritual vision comes into focus with the truth. We see that we are not losing. In fact, the battle has already been won. We win!

Revival has already begun. There is no need to walk in gloom and doom or fear and anxiety. With our eyes off the enemy and on Christ with whom we are seated in the heavenly places, we can rejoice in peace while we occupy the land. As we go through life aware of God's presence and the power and authority that are ours, instead of the world impacting us, we will impact the world.

WHO I AM IN CHRIST

- I am a child of God (Rom. 8:16)

- I am not my own; I have been bought with a price (1 Cor. 6:19–20).

- I am crucified with Christ (Gal. 2:20).

- I am Christ's radiant bride, without spot or wrinkle (2 Cor. 11:2).

- I am redeemed and forgiven of my sins (Col. 1:13–14).

- I am the righteousness of God in Christ (2 Cor. 5:21).

- I am complete in Christ (Col. 2:10).

- I am significant (1 Cor. 12:27).

- I am a citizen of heaven (Phil. 3:18–21).

- I am part of the body of Christ (1 Cor. 12:12–14).

- I am deeply loved by God (1 John 4:10).

- I am called by name (Isa. 43:1).

- I am saved by grace through faith (Eph. 2:8).

- I am a friend of God, chosen by Him and appointed to bear good fruit (John 15:15–16).

- I am washed in the blood of Jesus (Rev. 1:5).

- I am sanctified and justified (1 Cor. 6:11).

- I am a new creation in Christ, and all things have become new (2 Cor. 5:17).

- I am God's workmanship, created for good works (Eph. 2:10).

- I am a partaker of the divine nature (2 Pet. 1:4).

- I am in covenant with the Lord (Heb. 10:16).

- I am God's masterpiece (Eph. 2:10).

- I am holy (Heb. 3:1).

- I am made in the image of God (Gen. 1:26–27).

- I am full and complete, lacking nothing (Col. 2:9–10).

- I am redeemed from the curse of the Law (Gal. 3:13).

- I am delivered from the powers of darkness and translated into the kingdom of Jesus Christ (Col. 1:13).

- I am God's treasured possession (Exod. 19:5).

- I am His sheep and He is my Shepherd (Ps. 23:1).

- I am led by the Spirit of God (Rom. 8:14).

- I can do all things through Christ who strengthens me (Phil. 4:13).

- I am accepted in the Beloved (Eph. 1:6).

- I am an heir of God and joint heir with Jesus (Rom. 8:17).

- I am seated with Christ in heavenly places (Eph. 2:6).

- I am an inheritor of eternal life (1 John 5:11-12).

- I am blessed with all spiritual blessings (Eph. 1:3).

- I am healed by His stripes (Isa. 53:5).

- I am prosperous (3 John 2).

- I am seated with Christ above principalities and powers (Eph. 1:19-21).

- I am above only and not beneath (Deut. 28:13).

- I am more than a conqueror (Rom. 8:37).

- I am an overcomer by the blood of the Lamb and the word of my testimony (Rev. 12:11).

NOTES

CHAPTER 3

1. Blue Letter Bible, s.v. *"paraklētos,"* accessed December 22, 2022, https://www.blueletterbible.org/lexicon/g3875/kjv/tr/0-1/.

CHAPTER 4

1. Blue Letter Bible, s.v. *"deō,"* accessed December 22, 2022, https://www.blueletterbible.org/lexicon/g1210/kjv/tr/0-1/; Blue Letter Bible, s.v. *"lyō,"* accessed December 22, 2022, https://www.blueletterbible.org/lexicon/g3089/kjv/tr/0-1/.

CHAPTER 9

1. Glorious Church, *Smith Wigglesworth—The Secret of His Power by Albert Hibbert*, YouTube video, 1:11:53, August 14, 2017, https://www.youtube.com/watch?v=5pe7rvVvh_c.
2. C. H. Spurgeon, "The Ravens' Cry," transcript of sermon delivered at The Metropolitan Tabernacle, Newington, January 14, 1866, https://ccel.org/ccel/spurgeon/sermons12/sermons12.v.html.

CHAPTER 11

1. *Merriam-Webster*, s.v. "pillar," accessed December 22, 2022, https://www.merriam-webster.com/dictionary/pillar.
2. Blue Letter Bible, s.v. *"ekklēsia,"* accessed December 22, 2022, https://www.blueletterbible.org/lexicon/g1577/kjv/tr/0-1/.

CHAPTER 15

1. Blue Letter Bible, s.v. *"angelos,"* accessed December 22, 2022, https://www.blueletterbible.org/lexicon/g32/kjv/tr/0-1/.

CHAPTER 16

1. Windell Gann, "Commentary on Ephesians 1:3," Gann's Commentary on the Bible, accessed December 22, 2022, https://www.studylight.org/commentaries/gbc/ephesians-1.html.
2. Gann, "Commentary on Ephesians 1:3."
3. Kenneth S. Wuest, *Wuest's Word Studies From the Greek New Testament for the English Reader*, vol. 1 (Grand Rapids, MI: Wm. B. Eerdmans Publishing Company, 1973), 54.
4. Wuest, *Wuest's Word Studies From the Greek New Testament for the English Reader*, vol. 1, 54.
5. Blue Letter Bible, s.v. "*kratos*," accessed December 22, 2022, https://www.blueletterbible.org/lexicon/g2904/kjv/tr/0-1/.
6. Britannica, s.v. "Ecclesia," accessed December 22, 2022, https://www.britannica.com/topic/Ecclesia-ancient-Greek-assembly.

I pray this message will impact your life the way
it has mine.

—Mike Thompson

mikethompsonministries.org

*Rejoice always, pray without ceasing, in everything give
thanks; for this is the will of God in Christ Jesus for you.
Do not quench the Spirit. Do not despise prophecies. Test
all things; hold fast what is good. Abstain from every form
of evil. Now may the God of peace Himself sanctify you
completely; and may your whole spirit, soul, and body be
preserved blameless at the coming of our Lord Jesus Christ.*
—1 Thessalonians 5:16–23